THE SPIRIT HIMSELF BEARETH WITNESS

BY TOM HARMON

The Spirit Himself Beareth Witness

ISBN: 9781609200978
Printed in the United States of America
©2014 Tom Harmon
All rights reserved

Cover design by Ajoyin Publishing, Inc.
Front Cover Photo Joyce Harmon
Back Photo David DeJong
Proofed by Mary Evenson
Edited by Bob English
Interior design by Sunny B. DiMartino and Ajoyin Publishing, Inc.

API
Ajoyin Publishing, Inc.
P.O. 342
Three Rivers, MI 49093
www.ajoyin.com

Please direct your inquiries to admin@ajoyin.com

CONTENTS

FOREWORD

Oh the blessedness of the subject of the Holy Spirit of God. I don't know if it's possible to study the third person of the Godhead dispassionately. Careful study cannot help but bring about a doxological response. I kneel in awe and wonder at the single thought of the Holy Spirit dwelling within me. Selah.

The New Testament is full of accounts of the work of the Holy Spirit in the lives of believers. He is our teacher in the things of God, even revealing the deep things of God. He fills us and empowers us for service. He convicts us and comforts us. He is our personal guide in the way we should go. He never leads us in the wrong way but only in the liberating way of truth. He calls ministers and sends out workers. He intercedes for us, and seals us unto the day of redemption. He is the guarantee of our salvation and our proof that we are born of God. He is the promise of both the Father and the Son come true in our lives. He is the one who comes alongside us, not just to observe but to be the helper in our journey of faith. He is this and so much more.

May the Holy Spirit produce an abundant crop of His fruit as we give careful attention to this study. "But the fruit of the Spirit is love, joy, peace, long-suffering, gentleness, goodness, faith, meekness, self-control; against such there is no law." (Gal. 5:22–23).

PREFACE

I should be a better Christian than I am. I should be more spiritually mature, especially in relationship to the person and work of the Holy Spirit in my life. I have had many advantages: good Bible teachers, good learning resources, and some good godly examples. I know the fault does not lie with the faithful teaching ministry of the Holy Spirit but with my ability to hear with a spiritual ear and obey His voice. I have a lot to learn. I pray for a teachable spirit during this year's study, preaching and writing on the Holy Spirit.

The Spirit Himself beareth witness with our spirit, that we are the children of God. –Romans 8:16

CHAPTER ONE

THE PERSON OF GOD

It has been said that the highest thoughts a man can ever think are thoughts about God: Who He is, what He is like. We must realize that every problem we have in life is directly or indirectly related to our concept of God. God wants us to think rightly about Him so He has given us His resume, the Bible. God's Word explains the attributes of God. Each attribute is what God has revealed as being true about Himself. I hope it does not seem presumptuous to write of the person of God in one short chapter as though we could grasp the full understanding of Who He is and what He is like, yet sometimes, just a glimpse into His character gives us all we need for making right decisions in life.

GOD IS OMNISCIENT

To say that God is omniscient is to say that God knows everything. If someone knows everything he doesn't need to go to school or be taught. "Who hath directed the Spirit of the Lord, or being his counselor, hath taught him? With whom took he counsel, and who instructed him, and taught him in the path of justice, and taught him knowledge, and showed to him the way of understanding?" (Isa. 40:13–14). The answer to these rhetorical questions is obvious. Nobody has told God something He did not already know. He had no teacher and was never a pupil. I, on the other hand, had to learn everything I know. I had to learn how to roll over, crawl, sit up, stand up, take my first steps and eventually walk. I had to learn how to feed myself, learn how to speak the language of my parents, count, spell my name, tie my shoes; I even had to be potty trained and learn to dress myself. Everything I know I had to learn and I am still learning. However, God is omniscient, meaning He won't be any smarter this time next year than He is right now. This truth separates God and man. We would do well not to try and erase the line that puts God in a class all by Himself. He is God and I am Tom. He is infinitely wise and I have a lot to learn.

What I appreciate most about the omniscience of God is knowing that nobody can tattle on me to God. It is of the greatest comfort to my soul to know that He already knows all about me! There are no skeletons in my closet that God wasn't fully aware of when He called me to salvation and forgave me of all my sins. There were no unsuspected weaknesses or character flaws that He did not know. Oh how liberating it is to see God rightly and know that He loves me in spite of all He knows about me. It is comforting to know that even when I don't know my own mind, there is One who knows me altogether and has chosen me as His very own.

He knew the struggle I would have from time to time in forgetting who He really is and lapsing into thinking that He is something like me. "Thou thoughtest that I was altogether such an one as thyself" (Ps. 50:21b).

Maybe I shouldn't, but somehow I take comfort in knowing

that I'm not the only one who forgets that He is omniscient. A man by the name of Saul was on his way from Jerusalem to Damascus with a fist full of warrants to arrest Christians and bring them back for trial. The narrative is too good to leave out: "And as he journeyed, he came near Damascus, and suddenly there shone round about him a light from heaven; and he fell to the earth, and heard a voice saying unto him, Saul, Saul, why persecutest thou me? And he said, Who art thou, Lord? And the Lord said, I am Jesus, whom thou persecutest; it is hard for thee to kick against the goads. And he, trembling and astonished, said, Lord, what wilt thou have me to do? And the Lord said unto him, Arise, and go into the city, and it shall be told thee what thou must do. And the men who journeyed with him stood speechless, hearing a voice, but seeing no man. And Saul arose from the earth, and when his eyes were opened, he saw no man; but they led him by the hand, and brought him into Damascus. And he was there three days without sight, and neither did eat nor drink. And there was a certain disciple at Damascus, named Ananias; and to him said the Lord in a vision, Ananias. And he said, Behold, I am here, Lord. And the Lord said unto him, Arise, and go into the street which is called Straight, and inquire in the house of Judas for one called Saul, of Tarsus; for, behold, he prayeth, and hath seen in a vision a man, named Ananias, coming in and putting his hand on him, that he might receive his sight" (Acts 9:3–12).

I must preface the next two verses: Ananias is a disciple of the Lord, a good disciple, good enough that the Lord would speak to him and trust him to obey His voice. I love his response—it's so like us. Capture the scene with your sanctified imagination. "Then Ananias answered, Lord, I have heard by many of this man, how much evil he hath done to thy saints at

Jerusalem; And here he hath authority from the chief priests to bind all that call on thy name" (Acts 9:13–14). Was Ananias expecting God to say, "Oh thank you Ananias, I wasn't aware of this information, why if it hadn't been for you I might have chosen the wrong man; thank you for helping me be God." The Lord knows we sometimes forget His omniscience and He graciously encourages us to do what He asks.

When looking at the attributes of God they are all equally perfect and we should not hold one above another., Therefore I will not have a favorite, but if I did have a favorite, it may well be omniscience. His omniscience stirs me to wonder, awe, marvel, and ultimately worship. Sometimes it's nothing more than a speechless adoration. "Before I formed thee in the womb, I knew thee" (Jer. 1:5a).

GOD IS OMNIPRESENT

Omnipresence means that God is everywhere present. The psalmist writes: "Whither shall I go from thy Spirit? Or whither shall I flee from thy presence? If I ascend up into heaven, thou art there; if I make my bed in sheol, behold, thou art there. If I take the wings of the morning, and dwell in the uttermost parts of the sea, even there shall thy hand lead me, and thy right hand shall hold me. If I say, surely the darkness shall cover me; even the night shall be light about me. Yea, the darkness hideth not from thee, but the night shineth as the day; the darkness and the light are both alike to thee" (Ps. 139:7–12).

What about the darkness, or the dark days of life? Since the beginning of this year we have experienced several tragedies where one might be tempted to ask; where was God when all this was going on? A godly young father dies of a heart attack, leaving his wife and three teenage children behind.

A godly pastor kisses his daughter goodbye as she gets in the car and heads back to college. The weather gets bad and she dies in an automobile crash. A young wife with a seven week old baby complains of a headache and tells her husband she is going to the bedroom to lie down. Her husband checks on her an hour later to find her dead. The cause of death is a brain aneurysm. I received a call earlier today asking for prayer for a young couple that just lost their four month old baby to crib death.

We tend to focus only where we are at the time. We need to have the proper picture of God and who He is. He is omnipresent! He is with the young father in his final steps of life. He is with the pastor's daughter in the car crash. He is with the young mother as she takes her final breath. He is in the room with the four month old child. He's there. "Fear thou not; for I am with thee. Be not dismayed; for I am thy God. I will strengthen thee; yea, I will help thee; I will uphold thee with the right hand of my righteousness" (Isa. 41:10).

Job and his wife lost all ten of their children in one day to a horrible storm. The children were having a siblings' gathering in their eldest brother's home when a freak storm struck destroying the house, crushing them all to death. Job's wealth was gone the same day. He was left with only a handful of employees that he could no longer afford. He comes down with a rare, painful, disease of sore boils that cover him from head to toe. His wife can't take the trauma of it all, so she suggests that God has abandoned him and he should commit suicide and end it all. Three of his closest friends turn on him and begin accusing him of secret sins. They say God has found him out and this is His judgment on him. Where is God in all of this? He's there.

What about all the horrible atrocities that have happened

throughout time? From wars on the global scale, genocide, ethnic cleansing, persecution and suffering at the hands of evil men. Where was God during the holocaust under Hitler? Where was God during the sexual, mental, emotional abuse of a child? The answer remains the same: He was there. Rest assured., Because He was there in the past, He is here in the present, and He will be there in the future. The omnipresent God is an eye witness to every action both good and evil. He will one day make all things right. "Dearly beloved, avenge not yourselves but, rather, give place unto wrath; for it is written, Vengeance is mine; I will repay, saith the Lord" (Rom. 12:19). The omnipresence of God is both sobering and comforting.

How does the omnipresence of God affect me in the days of light? Prior to Job's great trial, things were going well for Job. God seemed to be blessing all he did. Some of the great men and women of God have a genuine embrace of the omnipresence of God and live as to do that which is right in the sight of the Lord. A healthy consciousness of the omnipresence of God leads to a more godly life and lends great advantage to our faith during times of temptation. Joseph was keenly aware of the presence of God. He had risen to a place of trusted authority in Potiphar's house. Potiphar's wife had cast her eyes upon young Joseph desiring him to be immoral with her. She told him the house was empty and she had sent all the servants away. Joseph knew God was present and he made a clear refusal, "How then can I do this great wickedness, and sin against God?" (Gen.39:9c).

I also find great consolation in the omnipresence of God, especially when we are traveling. "God is our refuge and strength, a very present help in trouble" (Ps. 46:1) Regardless of the state or country we are in, it is a comfort to know that

God is already there. The God of the Bible is fully present in China, India, Africa, Australia, Russia, Canada, Iran, Iraq, Israel, Mexico, North America, South America, and in every country, on every continent, on islands, in deserts, among tribal people, or in crowded cities. He is there! What a blessing to know that help is already present everywhere I go.

God Is Omnipotent

To say that God is omnipotent is to say that God has all power. To say that He has all power places Him in a class all His own. God earned the right to this description at creation. "Thou, even thou, art Lord alone; thou hast made heaven, the heaven of heavens, with all their host, the earth, and all things that are in it, the seas, and all that is in them, and thou preservest them all; and the host of heaven worshipeth thee" (Neh. 9:6). God created all things in six days and on the seventh day He rested. God made man in His likeness, making him unique and above all He had created. In His sovereign good pleasure He chose to rule the earth by giving man dominion over earth while at the same time maintaining authority over man. God makes the rules; the forbidden tree was "the rules". To rule, one must have power; to rule sovereignly, one must have all power. God gave Adam, or man, power; He even gave Satan and his demons power; but He didn't give it freely without accountability. Very few can be trusted with the dangerous commodity of power and nobody but God can be trusted with all power. He alone is the Almighty God. "Ah, Lord God! Behold, thou hast made the heaven and the earth by thy great power and outstretched arm, and there is nothing too hard for thee" (Jer. 32:17).

Because God created all things, He has the right to rule all things. "Hath not the potter power over the clay" (Rom.

9:21a). If God did not create us, He has no right to rule us; if He has no right to rule us, He has no right to judge us; and if He has no right to judge us, then the cross of Christ is absolutely meaningless because that is exactly what God did on the cross. He judged our sin in the person of His Son. "But we preach Christ crucified, unto the Jews a stumbling block, and unto the Gentiles foolishness; but unto them who are called, both Jews and Greeks, Christ the power of God, and the wisdom of God. Because the foolishness of God is wiser than men; and the weakness of God is stronger than men" (1 Cor. 1:23–25). Creation is one declaration of His omnipotence, the cross of Christ is another.

The final declaration of His omnipotence will be the return of Christ at the end of the age. The power of world kingdoms and rulers, and even the power of the devil, will be judged in righteousness by the one who sits on the throne. The Old Testament speaks of God's omnipotence as well as the New. "Remember the former things of old; for I am God, and there is none else; I am God, and there is none like me, declaring the end from the beginning, and from ancient times the things that are not yet done, saying, My counsel shall stand, and I will do all my pleasure" (Isa. 46:9–10). "And I heard, as it were, the voice of a great multitude, and like the voice of many waters, and like the voice of mighty peals of thunder, saying, Hallelujah! For the Lord God omnipotent reigneth" (Rev. 19:6). "And the seventh angel sounded; and there were great voices in heaven, saying, The kingdom of this world is become the kingdom of our Lord, and of his Christ, and he shall reign forever and ever" (Rev. 11:15). The entire Hallelujah chorus is but an obscure half note in comparison to the praise of which our omnipotent God is worthy.

GOD IS SELF-EXISTANT

The words "genesis" and "beginnings" apply to humans. They do not apply to God. When confronted with this truth, faith alone is allowed to enter; reason must kneel reverently outside. Faith must precede all attempts to reason especially as we consider the next three attributes of God.

When Moses saw the burning bush and went to investigate, at a certain distance the voice of God spoke to him telling him to take off his shoes for the ground he was on was holy ground. God further told Moses to return to Egypt and command Pharaoh to let the children of Israel go. Moses responded with "who am I that I should go unto Pharaoh?" My question is, "Who cares who Moses is?" What matters is Who is the God that is sending him.

When the Apostle Paul heard the voice of God on the Damascus road, he asked the right question. "Who are you, Lord?" After Jesus answered, Paul's next question was, "what do you want me to do?" The proper question is always: Who are you, Lord? The question of who we are is irrelevant.

When Moses finally decided to go deliver God's message to Pharaoh, he asked God this question: "And Moses said unto God, Behold, when I come unto the children of Israel, and shall say unto them, The God of your fathers hath sent me unto you; and they shall say to me, What is his name? what shall I say unto them? And God said unto Moses, I AM THAT I AM: and he said, Thus shalt thou say unto the children of Israel, I AM hath sent me unto you" (Ex. 3:13–14). God was existent based on His own existence, so unlike us.

By faith we understand things that are beyond our fallen capacity to comprehend. Let God be true and every man a liar. He is God and we are not. I am reminded of a statement I read on the T-shirt of a young man. As he was coming toward me the T-shirt read, "There is a God!" As he passed I turned to read the back, which said "And you are not Him!" Part of the curse is my affinity to humanize deity. I must be content to let God be Who He says He is.

There are those who promote that we came from nothing. If we came from nothing then it would be impossible to have evolved. Evolution depends on something from which it can evolve. When pressed, the evolutionist will say that we originated from microscopic dust particles far away in space. A logical question would seem, where did the particles come from; and for that matter, where did the space come from? There must be a source. Regardless of how many billions of years, evolution has to have a source from which to evolve. Nothing is self-existent but God. This is one of those attributes that draws a clear line of distinction between God and man. It puts Him in a class all His own and we would do well not to erase the line that separates Him from us.

GOD IS SELF-SUFFICIENT

To say that God is self-sufficient is to say He has no needs. On the other hand, I am constantly needy and complain when those needs are not met, e.g. I'm hot, I'm cold, I'm tired, I'm hungry, I'm thirsty, I'm lonely, etc. etc. etc. "If I were hungry, I would not tell thee; for the world is mine, and the fullness thereof" (Ps. 50:12).

As the Apostle Paul walked the streets of Athens alone his spirit was greatly moved for he saw the people wholly given to idolatry. Everywhere he looked he saw fetishes and little shrines to all kinds of man-made gods. He began to preach Christ and some of the learned religious men invited him to speak on Mar's Hill at their regular formal gathering. Let's pick up the narrative: "Then Paul stood in the midst of Mars Hill, and said, Ye men of Athens, I perceive that in all things ye are very religious. For as I passed by, and beheld your devotions, I found an altar with the inscription, TO THE UNKNOWN GOD, Whom, therefore, ye ignorantly worship, him declare I unto you. God, who made the world and all things in it, seeing that he is Lord of heaven and earth, dwelleth not in temples made with hands, neither is worshiped with men's hands, as though he needed anything, seeing he giveth to all life, and breath, and all things" (Acts 17:22–25). In my feeble attempts to humanize deity I have actually had moments of insanity when I thought that God might even need me. God is self-sufficient and needs nothing in order for Him to be God, not even me!

As I study God I must always see Him bigger than my theology. I too often hastily construct a theological shack made of papier-mâché and expect Him to dwell in it. When Solomon began to build the temple in Jerusalem he asked himself this question: "But who is able to build him an house, seeing the heaven and heaven of heavens cannot contain him? Who am I, then, that I should build him an house, except only to burn sacrifice before him?" (2Chr. 2:6). At this point Solomon is humbly on track with proper theology. It is obvious since he mentions the heaven of heavens that the first heaven we see by day, the second heaven we see by night, and the third heaven we see by faith. The third heaven or heaven of heavens is the dwelling place of God; He is in heaven and we are upon earth. We dare not try and erase the line that separates the greatness of God from the frailty of man.

GOD IS ETERNAL

Scripture records numerous times the phrases, "and it came to pass" or "in the process of time". Neither of these statements applies to the person of God. Man on the other hand is born in time. From the beginning of time until the end of time man's life is but one grain of sand on the seashores of eternity. Even that is not an accurate description because there is a fixed number of grains of sand and they could conceivably be counted, but eternity has no such limit. "Lord, thou hast been our dwelling place in all generations. Before the mountains were brought forth, or ever thou hadst formed the earth and the world, even from everlasting to everlasting, thou art God" (Ps. 90:1–2). Simply said, God has no circumference. He cannot be measured or reduced to time alone. God operates in time but always from the vantage point of eternity. "Now unto the King eternal, immortal, invisible, the only wise God, be honor and glory forever and ever. Amen" (1 Tim.1:17).

Man's life is short at best. If he lives to be a hundred or even if he could live to be a thousand, it would go by him in a blur. David compared man's life to a handbreadth. If you get your threescore and ten or by reason of strength fourscore (70 or 80 years) at the end of your arm you can see your entire life from birth to death just by observing the width of your hand. As David is considering the fact that the wood of the cradle rubs tightly against the marble of the tomb he seems for a moment almost depressed. He knows it is something he must consider but is reluctant to do so. "Lord, make me to know mine end, and the measure of my days, what it is that I may know how frail I am. Behold, thou hast made my days as an handbreadth, and mine age is as nothing before thee. Verily every man at his best state is altogether vanity. Selah. Surely every man walketh in a vain show; surely they are disquieted in vain; he heapeth up riches and knoweth not who shall gather them" (Ps. 39:4–6) For a moment vanity begins settling in on David. Vanity is the emptiness of trying to be happy without God. He is rescued from the vanity which comes from contemplating the short time of his life by looking at the eternality of God. "And now, Lord, what wait I for? My hope is in thee" (v7).

My favorite word is eternity. I love the very sound of the word. It restores perspective when time alone would steal the bigger picture. Anyone who thinks well on the truth of eternity will trouble himself little with what happens in these three or four moments of temporal life. "So teach us to number our days, that we may apply our hearts unto wisdom" (Ps. 90:12). "For thus sayeth the high and lofty One who inhabiteth eternity, whose name is Holy; I dwell in the high and holy place, with him also who is of a contrite and humble spirit, to revive the spirit of the humble, and to revive the heart of the contrite ones"(Isa. 57:15).

To be humble and contrite is to be teachable. I have a lot to learn about the truth that God has been our dwelling place in all generations and will continue to dwell with us. Oh that I might see God as high and lifted up. To my shame I too often have too low of an opinion of God and too high an opinion of myself. Too often my nose is glued to one tile on the mosaic and I lose the beauty of the bigger picture. I need to step back and take a look at the glories of eternity. "And, as Moses lifted up the serpent in the wilderness, even so must the Son of man be lifted up; that whosoever believeth in him should not perish, but have eternal life. For God so loved the world, that he gave his only begotten Son, that whosoever believeth in him should not perish, but have everlasting life" (Jn. 3:14–16).

GOD IS IMMUTABLE

To say that God is immutable is to say that He does not change. "For I am the Lord, I change not" (Mal. 3:6a). God Himself changes things but He Himself does not change. He doesn't get better or worse. We do both. We live in a world of constant change, some for the better, and some for the worse. The immutability of God is important in all things but especially as we consider the hope of the gospel. What if God were to suddenly change the gospel from salvation by grace through faith to salvation by works and the keeping of the law? How would we do when stacked up against the righteous standard of the law? The truth of the Law is that it demands perfection. "For whosoever shall keep the whole law, and yet offend in one point, he is guilty of all" (Jas. 2:10).

The Pharisees of Jesus' day were bent on keeping the Law as a means of entrance into heaven. They knew they couldn't keep it perfectly but they thought their best shot would probably be sufficient. They had the Law memorized but they missed the truth of the Law: perfection. You can't murder in moderation, or steal, or lie, or commit adultery. You can't even covet or your hopes of righteousness under the Law collapse.

The Apostle Paul was a Pharisee and the son of a Pharisee. He was generationally deep into the legalism of the Pharisees. He was a good guy and under the Law, in his eyes, he was righteous before God. I believe he acknowledged only one God and it was the right one, Yahweh. I believe he would use His Name in only a respectful and honoring way. He would never esteem an idol of any kind for he believed in the invisible God. He rested on the Sabbath and would even go the extra mile. He honored his parents as evidenced in honoring their wishes as he went off to boarding school and learned at the feet of the best Pharisee of his day, Gamaliel (see Acts 22:3). I believe he was a man of his word and could be trusted with someone else's property. He would not have considered himself a murderer or someone who could be bought. His own testimony bears evidence of his pre-grace days. "Though I might also have confidence in the flesh. If any other man thinketh that he hath reasons for which he might trust in the flesh, I more: Circumcised the eighth day, of the stock of Israel, of the tribe of Benjamin, an Hebrew of the Hebrews; as touching the law, a Pharisee; concerning zeal, persecuting the church; touching the righteousness which is in the law, blameless" (Phil.3:4–6).

The problem is not with the Law for Paul also wrote: "Wherefore, the law is holy, and the commandment holy, and just, and good" (Rom. 7:12). In fact it was the last commandment that sank Paul's pharisaical ship. "Thou shall not covet" brought him to his knees. Covetousness lives quite comfortably in the dim regions of a religious heart. It may have taken him three years in the deserts of Arabia to learn it, but it was worth it. Covetousness deals with the heart and most people acknowledge that the heart of the matter is always the matter of the heart. Paul's motives under the Law weren't as pure as he thought they were. Paul came to grips with his self-righteousness under the Law and placed his hope in the gospel of grace; that same gospel of imputed righteousness which Abraham, David and all the Old Testament saints had found.

The writer of Hebrews records God's unchangeable character this way: "That by two immutable things, in which it was impossible for God to lie, we might have a strong consolation, who have fled for refuge to lay hold upon the hope set before us, which hope we have as an anchor of the soul, both sure and steadfast, and which entereth into that within the veil" (Heb.

6:18–19). What a blessing to know that God does not change, that He is immutable. He will never change His mind from Christ's work to mine. If this is the way God is, I think it is safe to say it's because it's the way He has always been, and if it's the way He's always been, it's the way He will always be. "Jesus Christ, the same yesterday, and today, and forever" (Heb. 13:8).

It seems a perfect spot for a great old hymn of praise. It was written by the godly pastor/evangelist, A. B. Simpson.

Oh, how sweet the glorious message simple faith may claim;
Yesterday, today, forever, Jesus is the same; Still He loves to save the sinful, heal the sick and lame,
Cheer the mourner, still the tempest-glory to His name!

Yesterday, today, forever, Jesus is the same,
All may change, but Jesus never-glory to His name!
Glory to His name! Glory to His name!
All may change, but Jesus never-glory to His name!

GOD IS JUST

Many times I have heard people say that God is not fair. Each time I hear it, I rejoice in my spirit and give thanks to God that He is not fair. If He were fair all of us would suffer the judgment of eternal punishment for our sins. When you think of fairness, consider an umpire who stands behind the plate calling a game. He gives his very best to call a perfect game. One small distraction, one momentary lapse of concentration may affect his judgment and make him call a close pitch either way. It could have been a ball or it could have been a strike. He wants to be fair so he reasons: "If another one comes across the plate close to the same area, I'll make up for it with the opposite call and kind of equal it all out." Can you imagine God with the same attitude? He sends one to Hell on a close call and to be fair He reasons, "I'll make up for it on the next one by sending him to Heaven." When God makes a judgment, you can count on it to be exactly what it is. There are no people making it to heaven on a close call or what is often thought by the skin of their teeth. They are either completely perfectly justified, or they are totally condemned and eternally lost. No close calls and nothing fair about it.

When God deals with sinful man you can be sure it is with perfect justice. "He is the Rock, his work is perfect; for all his ways are justice; a God of truth and without iniquity, just and right is he" (Deut. 32:4). Every man will one day stand before God and give and account of his actions. We will not stand before a jury of our peers; neither will there be any plea deals on the table to negotiate. The Judge before whom we will stand cannot be deceived or bribed. He has always been this way even before Adam and Eve in the garden. If the Judge who made the law about the forbidden tree would have winked at their transgression, He would have ceased to be God. Even Abraham knew and understood the justice of God when he said, "Shall not the Judge of all the earth do right?" (Gen. 18:25c). It is of extreme importance that God is just. For if He weren't He could not be merciful, gracious, and loving.

GOD IS MERCIFUL, GRACIOUS, AND LOVING

Mercy is God not doing to us what we deserve because we deserve justice and judgment. If I were just before God according to His demands I would need no mercy. I could stand before the Judge of all the earth without fear of guilt. But if I am honest with my own conscience and soul, I know I cannot defend myself on the merits of my own case and must hope for mercy. Justice must be served if God is to remain just. That was exactly what God did at the cross when He sent His only Son as a payment for the penalty of my crimes. His Son was righteous under the Law for He met the perfect demands of God's justice. In the mercy of God, justice was satisfied by the substitutionary death of Christ. His uprightness for our guilt, once and for all, to everyone who believes in Jesus as their only hope of eternal life. The gospel is not what we have done for God, but what God, in His mercy, has done for us. "For Christ also hath once suffered for sins, the just for the unjust, that he might bring us to God, being put to death in the flesh, but made alive by the Spirit" (1 Pet. 3:18) The righteous standard of God's justice could only be met by His own righteous doing. He alone gets the glory because in His mercy He has shown us grace by which we can be declared righteous or just before Him. Mercy is God not doing something to us that we do deserve.

Grace, on the other hand, is God doing something for us that we don't deserve. Grace is the divine enabling power of God that draws us to Christ, reveals the truth of the gospel and gives us the faith to believe it. "Being justified freely by his grace through the redemption that is in Christ Jesus, whom God hath set forth to be a propitiation through faith in his blood, to declare his righteousness for the remission of sins that are past, through the forbearance of God; to declare, I say, at this time his righteousness, that he might be just, and the justifier of him who believeth in Jesus. Where is boasting then? It is excluded. By what law? Of works? Nay, but by the law of faith. Therefore, we conclude that a man is justified by faith apart from the deeds of the law" (Rom. 3:24–28).

If we can understand the justice, mercy, and grace of God,

and I think we can, we can even trace the logic of who, what, how, when and where this all played out.

Who?	Jesus
What?	The sacrifice for sin
How?	The cross of Calvary
When?	Approximately 2000 years ago
Where?	Jerusalem
Why?	Ah, the "why" questions about God are always

the hardest to answer. The only answer found in Scripture is—He loved us. Ok, why did He love us? It was certainly not because we are so loveable. "In which in times past ye walked according to the course of this world, according to the prince of the power of the air, the spirit that now worketh in the sons of disobedience; Among whom also we all had our manner of life in times past in the lust of our flesh, fulfilling the desires of the flesh and of the mind, and were by nature the children of wrath, even as others. But God, who is rich in mercy, for his great love with which he loved us, even when we were dead in sins, hath made us alive together with Christ (by grace ye are saved), and hath raised us up together, and made us sit together in heavenly places in Christ Jesus; that in the ages to come he might show the exceeding riches of his grace in his kindness toward us through Christ Jesus. For by grace are ye saved through faith; and that not of yourselves, it is the gift of God—Not of works, lest any man should boast" (Eph. 2:2–9).

In John's gospel the writer often refers to himself as the disciple whom the Lord loved. It was as if he couldn't get over the fact that God genuinely loved him. His letters are filled with the love of God. Its effect on him was shown in his exhortations to the Church: "Beloved, let us love one another; for love is of God, and everyone that loveth is born of God, and knoweth God. He that loveth not knoweth not God; for God is love. In this was manifested the love of God toward us, that God sent his only begotten Son into the world, that we might live through him. Herein is love, not that we loved God, but that he loved us, and sent his Son to be the propitiation for our sins" (1 Jn. 4:7–10).

Throughout the life and ministry of the Apostle Paul, he too, could never get over the fact that God loved him, he who had been a persecutor of the Church and an Ex-Christian killer. He looked upon the sufferings and hardships he faced while serving the Lord as not even worthy of comparison with the love Christ showered on him. "For the love of Christ constraineth us" (2 Cor. 5:14a). Paul is not talking about his love for Christ but about Christ's love for him. The small preposition "of" means to proceed from a source. God initiated and committed His love for Paul, not vice versa. If we love God, it's because He first loved us.

The question is, and will always remain, why? I find solace in the only answer: it's because it's the way He is, and if it's the way He is, it's safe to say it's because it's the way He's always been. And if it's the way He's always been, it's the way He'll always be—immutable!

GOD IS HOLY

Most people have some natural understanding of justice, mercy, grace, and love; but we are absolutely void of any concept of holiness. We dare not say God is holy because He conforms to some standard. He is the standard. The very word "holy" is deserving of serious contemplation and respect. Holiness is what makes God incomprehensible and terrifyingly unapproachable. The warning of God to Moses at Sinai was clear, "When I come

24

down to the mountain to speak with you, tell the people not to get to close, and for sure don't touch the mountain or else they will die." If there is ever an attribute of God that should sober us and cause us to tremble, it is the holiness of God.

In a vision, God gave Isaiah a glimpse of His holiness. That momentary experience would radically affect the rest of his life. He was instantly aware of his utter depravity and woeful condition. He would have run but he was undone and paralyzed with fear. If God didn't intervene soon he would surely perish. Oh how unholy and profane he must have felt. He was a priest and had been leading the people in worship and prayer for 23 years and he was no better than the worst of them; he was right in the middle with them. In a sense he was face to face with God observing true worship and he was sickened at what he had been offering as worship. He felt as though he would be vaporized if God didn't show mercy quickly. His record says it best: "In the year that King Uzziah died, I saw also the Lord sitting upon a throne, high and lifted up, and his train filled the temple. Above it stood the seraphim: each one had six wings; with two he covered his face, and with two he covered his feet, and with two he did fly. And one cried unto another, and said, Holy, holy, holy, is the Lord of hosts; the whole earth is full of his glory. And the posts of the door moved at the voice of him who cried, and the house was filled with smoke. Then said I, Woe is me! For I am undone, because I am a man of unclean lips, and I dwell in the midst of a people of unclean lips; for mine eyes have seen the King, the Lord of hosts. Then flew one of the seraphim unto me, having a live coal in his hand, which he had taken with the tongs from off the altar. And he laid it upon my mouth, and said, Lo, this hath touched thy lips, and thine iniquity is taken away, and thy sin purged. Also I heard the voice of the Lord, saying, Whom shall I send, and who will go for us? Then said I, Here am I; send me" (Isa. 6:1–8).

Everything about God is holy. His Word is holy. "Paul, a servant of Jesus Christ, called to be an apostle, separated unto the gospel of God (Which he had promised before by his prophets in the holy scriptures)" (Rom 1:1–2). His Son is Holy. "Then said Mary unto the angel, How shall this be, seeing I know not a man? And the angel answered, and said unto her, The Holy Spirit shall come upon thee, and the power of the Highest shall overshadow thee; therefore also that holy thing which shall be born of thee shall be called the Son of God" (Lk. 1:34–35). The third person of the Godhead, the Spirit of God is likewise holy. He is named the Holy Spirit of whom the remainder of this book will focus.

CHAPTER TWO

THE SPIRIT HIMSELF

Who is the Holy Spirit? In order to answer this question we must continue with our look at the person of God. God is three persons, each fully God, and yet He is one God. This truth is often referred to as the trinity or the tri-unity of God. This teaching is foundational to who the Holy Spirit is, what He is like, where He lives, and how He works in the world today. It is so important to carefully (rightly) divide this truth. Many errors in the Christian religion can be traced back to a wrong view of this doctrine. As we proceed, let me say in advance: there will forever remain a mystery connected to this divine truth. I am not discouraged for He has been pleased to reveal enough Scriptures for us to press on and come to an understanding.

WHAT SAYETH THE SCRIPTURES

Every word of Scripture is holy and inspired of God. As the Apostle Paul was writing New Testament Scripture, he would often refer to an Old Testament text asking, "For what saith the scripture?" (Rom. 4:3). Then he would use accounts of Abraham or David as illustrations showing the continuity of the gospel between the Old and New Testaments. God used human authors while not impairing their intelligence, or personal experience, or their particular literary style. God supernaturally directed the writing of Scripture so that they recorded with perfect accuracy God's complete and infallible revelation to man. If God had written the Scriptures with His own hand, it could not have been more accurate or authoritative than it is now. Paul emphasized this in his last words to his son in the faith, Timothy. "And that from a child thou hast known the holy scriptures, which are able to make thee wise unto salvation through faith which is in Christ Jesus. All scripture is given by inspiration of God, and is profitable for doctrine, for reproof, for correction, for instruction in righteousness, that the man of God may be perfect, thoroughly furnished unto all good works" (2 Tim. 3:15–17). Though the Scriptures never mention the word trinity, the tri-unity of God is clearly taught in its pages.

THE PLURALITY OF GOD

In the book of Genesis we begin to see the plurality of God. "And God said, Let us make man in our image, after our likeness" (Gen. 1:26a). There is a basic convention in all languages to differentiate between one and more than one, singular and plural. This is often mirrored in the pronouns like "me" vs "us" or "my" vs "ours". If I were to say, "I love my wife", no problem; but if I were to say "I love our wife", we have a problem. When God set out to create man He made it clear. By saying that man would be made in Our image, after Our likeness, He was saying we would be made like Them.

After the fall of man it says, "And the Lord God said, Behold, the man is become as one of us" (Gen 3:22a). After the flood man was still determined to make his own way to God so he began building a tower to heaven. At that time there was only one language. Communication is one of man's greatest assets on any project. God stopped the project and this is how He did it, "Come, let us go down, and there confound their language, that they may not understand one another's speech" (Gen. 11:7). Also in the days of Isaiah the prophet, God refers to Himself in the plural. "Also I heard the voice of the Lord, saying, Whom shall I send, and who will go for us? Then said I, Here am I; send me" (Isa. 6:8).

ONE GOD

In the book of Deuteronomy Moses reviews Israel's history after their exodus from Egypt. The Egyptians had worshiped many gods. The people of the land to which they were going to possess also worshiped many gods. The Israelites, however, would worship only one God. "Hear, O Israel: The Lord our God is one Lord; And thou shalt love the Lord thy God with all thine heart, and with all thy soul, and with all thy might" (Dt. 6:4–5).

In the New Testament it's recorded that a scribe came to Jesus and asked him which was the most important commandment of all. The scribe made his living making copies of the Old Testament and knew well the words of Moses. Jesus quoted to him Deuteronomy 6:4–5 and also added, "love your neighbor as yourself." "And the scribe said unto him, Well, Master, thou hast said the truth; for there is one God, and there is no other but he. And to love him with all the heart, and with all the understanding, and with all the soul, and with all the strength, and to love his neighbor as himself, is more than all whole burnt offering and sacrifices. And when Jesus saw that he answered discreetly, he said unto him, Thou art not far from the kingdom of God. And no man after that dared to ask him any question" (Mk.12:32–34).

Paul speaks of God's Oneness: "For there is one God, and one mediator between God and men, the man, Christ Jesus" (1 Tim. 2:5). Paul's letter to the church in Ephesus is rich in basic doctrine and he drives home the teaching of one God. "There is one body, and one Spirit, even as ye are called in one hope of your calling; One Lord, one faith, one baptism, One God and Father us all, who is above all, and through you all, and in you all" (Eph. 4:4–6).

ONE GOD IN THREE PERSONS

At the baptism of Jesus the plurality of God is witnessed. "And Jesus, when he was baptized, went up straightway out of the water; and, lo, the heavens were opened unto him, and he saw the Spirit of God descending like a dove, and lighting upon him. And, lo, a voice from heaven, saying, This is my beloved Son, in whom I am well pleased" (Mt. 3:16–17).

At what is referred to as the Great Commission, Jesus gave His disciples these instructions: "Go ye, therefore, and teach all nations, baptizing them in the name of the Father, and of the Son, and of the Holy Spirit, teaching them to observe all things whatsoever I have commanded you; and, lo, I am with you always, even unto the end of the age. Amen' (Mt. 28:19–20).

The Apostle Paul signs off his second letter to the church of Corinth by naming each of the three Persons of the Godhead. "The grace of the Lord Jesus Christ, and the love of God, and the communion of the Holy Spirit be with you all. Amen" (2Cor. 13:14).

The Church was already well established throughout the world when Jude wrote a powerful postcard epistle to the

Church at large. He sees heresies creeping in and undermining the faith of some. He encourages them to earnestly contend for the faith which was once delivered to the saints. Near the end of his letter he also makes reference to the Tri-Oneness of God: "But ye, beloved, building up yourselves on your most holy faith, praying in the Holy Spirit, keep yourselves in the love of God, looking for the mercy of our Lord Jesus Christ unto eternal life" (Jude 20–21). At the end of Jude he records a doxological response to the tri-oneness of God. "Now unto him that is able to keep you from falling, and to present you faultless before the presence of his glory with exceeding joy, to the only wise God our Savior, be glory and majesty, dominion and power, both now and ever. Amen" (Jude 24, 25). Good theology is always accompanied with praise.

THE DISCIPLES OF CHRIST AND THE TRINITY

Jesus taught his disciples also on the subject of the Trinity. He had many things to say to them but acknowledged the fact that they weren't able to bear them, but that after He had gone the Holy Spirit would teach them all things concerning Himself. We will consider just a few Scriptures from the gospel of John: "My sheep hear my voice, and I know them, and they follow me. And I give unto them eternal life; and they shall never perish, neither shall any man pluck them out of my hand. My Father, who gave them to me, is greater than all, and no man is able to pluck them out of my Father's hand. I and my Father are one" (Jn. 10:27–30). I'm not sure the disciples understood what He meant but the orthodox Jews knew what He was saying. "Then the Jews took up stones again to stone him. Jesus answered them, Many good works have I shown you from my Father; for which of those works do ye stone me? The Jews answered him, saying, For a good work we stone thee not, but for blasphemy; and because that thou, being a man, makest thyself God" (vv.31–33).

In John 14 Jesus had just told His disciples that He was leaving them and that they couldn't go with Him yet. Their hearts were heavy so He told them of His Father's house and the heavenly home He was going to prepare for them. When Jesus told them they had seen the Father, Phillip says, "just show us the Father and we will be satisfied." "If ye had known me, ye should have known my Father also; and from henceforth ye know him, and have seen him. Philip saith unto him, Lord, show us the Father, and it sufficeth us. Jesus saith unto him, Have I been such a long time with you, and yet hast thou not known me, Philip? He that hath seen me hath seen the Father; and how sayest thou then, Show us the Father?" (Jn. 14:7–9).

A few verses later Jesus said He would pray to the Father that He would give them another comforter, One that would abide with them forever. If they were struggling with Jesus and the Father being One what must they have thought when He told them of another One coming to take His place? "And I will pray the Father, and he shall give you another Comforter, that he may abide with you forever; Even the Spirit of truth, whom the world cannot receive, because it seeth him not, neither knoweth him; but ye know him; for he dwelleth with you, and shall be in you. I will not leave you comfortless; I will come to you" (vv.16–18). The Comforter is clearly identified some verses later. "But the Comforter, who is the Holy Spirit, whom the Father will send in my name, he shall teach you all things, and bring all things to your remembrance, whatever I have said unto you" (v.26). It is important to note that Jesus said that the Father would send Him. A couple of chapters later Jesus is again saying that He would send the Holy Spirit. "Nevertheless, I tell you the truth; It is expedient for you that I go away; for if I go not away, the Comforter will not come unto you; but if I depart, I will send him unto you" (16:7). Jesus is gently trying to tell them of the Godhead. God is three Persons; each fully God, yet He is one God. Is it any wonder He said to them, "I have many things to say unto you, but ye cannot bear them now" (v.12).

WHO RAISED JESUS FROM THE DEAD?

There are 15 references in the book of Acts that say that God (referring to the Father) raised Jesus from the dead. Let's look at just one. Peter is preaching his first Holy Spirit-anointed sermon on the day of Pentecost. The disciples are accused by the Pharisees of being drunk. Peter tells them it's only 9:00 am and these men are not drunk. He quotes the prophecy of Joel about the coming of the Holy Spirit. He then turns his attention toward the risen Lord Jesus: "Ye men of Israel, hear these words: Jesus of Nazareth, a man approved of God among you by miracles, and wonders and signs, which God did by him in the midst of you, as ye yourselves also know; Him, being delivered by the determinate counsel and foreknowledge of God, ye have taken, and by wicked hands have crucified and slain; Whom God hath raised up, having loosed the pains of death, because it was not possible that he should be held by it" (Acts 2:22–24).

Let's also consider two portions in Romans: "That if thou shalt confess with thy mouth the Lord Jesus, and shalt believe in thine heart that God hath raised him from the dead, thou shalt be saved" (Rom. 10:9). Two chapters earlier the Holy Spirit inspired Paul to write these words concerning the resurrection of Jesus: "But if the Spirit of him that raised up Jesus from the dead dwell in you, he that raised up Christ from the dead shall also give life to your mortal bodies by his Spirit that dwelleth in you" (Rom. 8:11).

When Pilate boasted to Jesus that he had the power to crucify Him or release Him, Jesus spoke up. "Jesus answered, Thou couldest have no power at all against me, except it were given thee from above" (Jn. 19:11a). Jesus had already made it clear that He was going to lay down His life and He would take it up again. "Therefore doth my Father love me, because I lay down my life, that I may take it again. No man taketh it from me, but I lay it down of myself. I have power to lay it down, and I have power to take it again. This commandment have I received of my Father. There was a division therefore again among the Jews for these sayings" (Jn. 10:17–19). So who raised Jesus from the dead? T-HE-Y did.

Scripture seems to indicate that all three Persons of the Godhead were responsible for raising Jesus from the dead. The Jewish people didn't have a problem with God the Father or even God the Holy Spirit; it was God the Son, the stumbling block with Whom they had a problem. When God took on flesh it was more than most people could imagine, let alone believe.

THE INCARNATE TRIUNE GOD

I have heard it said, if you want to know God in His fullness, the simplest and most straightforward way is to study Jesus. Remember, God is three Persons, each fully God, co-equal, co-eternal, co-powerful yet they have different functions while remaining one God. This is most clearly seen in the incarnation. "But, when the fullness of time was come, God sent forth his Son, made of a woman, made under the law, to redeem them

34

that were under the law, that we might receive the adoption of sons" (Gal. 4:4, 5). God sent the pre-incarnate Jesus to earth, and the Holy Spirit overshadowed the young Virgin Mary and she conceived in her womb the Son of God. When the angel Gabriel told Mary she was to have the Christ Child, in faith she wondered how it could be. "Then said Mary unto the angel, How shall this be, seeing I know not a man? And the angel answered, and said unto her, The Holy Spirit shall come upon thee, and the power of the Highest shall overshadow thee; therefore also that holy thing which shall be born of thee shall be called the Son of God" (Lk. 1:34–35).

"[Jesus] is the image of the invisible God, the first-born of all creation" (Col. 1:15). Jesus is also credited as having all the fullness of the Godhead in Himself bodily. "For in him dwelleth all the fullness of the Godhead bodily" (Col. 2:9). Jesus literally represents everything that is attributed to the one God of the Bible. The writer of Hebrews says that Jesus is the exact image of the Person of God Himself. "Who, being the brightness of his glory, and the express image of his person, and upholding all things by the word of his power, when he had by himself purged our sins, sat down on the right hand of the Majesty on high" (Heb.1:3).

THE SPIRIT HIMSELF

Jesus had sat down in heaven at the right hand of the Father, awaiting the trumpet of God announcing His promised return. Both the Father and the Son had promised the disciples that the Holy Spirit would come and stay with them even unto the end of the age. The Holy Spirit had been charged with great responsibility in the carrying out of the business of the Church. Rest assured He will complete His work. Being fully God He was in on the design of His assignments before the foundations of the world and will see it on into eternity. His general residence has always been with mankind because of His omnipresence, but something very personal was going to happen at Pentecost. The Holy Spirit was to dwell in the body of each individual who was born of the Sprit. His ministry, though continuing to be global, would now be accomplished through the individual lives of believers making up the greater body, which is the Church. His residence would be in our bodies. His ministry in us would confirm that we are the children of God. "The Spirit himself beareth witness with our spirit, that we are the children of God" (Rom. 8:16).

In our next chapter we will look at the significance of Pentecost and in the remaining chapters we will deal with His witness in the world through His personal work in our individual lives.

PENTECOST

"And when the day of Pentecost was fully come, they were all with one accord in one place. And suddenly there came a sound from heaven like a rushing mighty wind, and it filled the house where they were sitting. And there appeared unto them cloven tongues as of fire, and it sat upon each of them. And they were filled with the Holy Spirit, and began to speak with other tongues, as the Sprit gave them utterance" (Acts 2:1–4).

THE DAY HAD FINALLY ARRIVED

The timing of God is impeccable. The day of Pentecost was fully come. It wasn't a moment early or a moment late. Similar to the birth of Christ, the day was perfectly in time with God's eternal plan. "But, when the fullness of the time was come, God sent forth his Son, made of a woman, made under the law" (Gal. 4:4). The Jewish people had been waiting for centuries for their Messiah to come. Some had lost hope and wondered if He was ever coming at all. The day finally arrived and Christ was born in Bethlehem on the millisecond of perfect timing. There are those today who lose hope in the second coming of Christ, even mockers that say He won't return at all. No one knows the day or the hour, but one thing is certain: His return will be right on time. "For yet a little while, and he that shall come will come, and will not tarry" (Heb. 10:37).

Pentecost means fifty days and was established as a holiday long ago in the time of Moses and the wilderness wanderings. They were to count seven Sabbaths from the Feast of Passover. Then the next day they were to celebrate the Feast of Pentecost, also called the Feast of Weeks or the Feast of Harvest. The people would give a grain offering to God, not a tithe as under the Law, but as every man purposed in his heart. They were to give expressing their gratefulness to God for His goodness to them. "And ye shall count unto you from the next day after the Sabbath, from the day that ye brought the sheaf of the wave offering; seven Sabbaths shall be complete: Even unto the next day after the seventh Sabbath shall ye number fifty days; and ye shall offer a new meal offering unto the Lord" (Lev. 23:15–16).

The Pentecost we are now speaking of was precisely fifty days after the resurrection of Christ. The sheaf offering typified Christ and was offered without any leaven for there was no evil in Him. Fifty days later the new meal offering or offering of the loaves would typify the Church. The loaves would contain leaven because the Church, though redeemed, would still have sin in it. This offering of loaves would occur at the perfect moment in the early morning when the Day of Pentecost had fully come.

THE GLORIOUS CHURCH

The Sabbath day is the last day of the week, a day of rest established by God in the Genesis creation. The first day of the week then is Sunday. It was on the first day of the week that Jesus rose from the dead, Easter (or Resurrection) Sunday. It was also on the first day of the week that the Holy Spirit came at Pentecost. His coming transformed a Jewish feast into a Christian one. Sunday would become referred to as the Lord's Day as mentioned by John when exiled on Patmos: "I was in the Spirit on the Lord's day" (Rev. 1:10a). Pentecost was the birthday of the Church and it happened on a Sunday.

The Church would be made up of individuals in whom the Holy Spirit dwelt and they corporately would become a habitation of God through the Spirit. The Church would be built upon the foundation of the apostles and the prophets, Jesus Christ Himself being the Chief Cornerstone. "Now, therefore, ye are no more strangers and sojourners, but fellow citizens with the saints, and of the household of God; and are built upon the foundation of the apostles and prophets, Jesus Christ himself being the chief corner stone, in whom all the building fitly framed together groweth unto an holy temple in the Lord; in whom ye also are built together for an habitation of God through the Spirit" (Eph. 2:19–22).

The Church is not just some human institution like a social or political club where people gather for recreation and companionship. The Church belongs to Jesus as He clearly calls it in Scripture, My Church: "And I say also unto thee, That thou art Peter, and upon this rock I will build my church, and the gates of hades shall not prevail against it" (Mt. 16:18). Paul affirmed this truth when he appointed Timothy to set things in order in the churches of Asia. As an apostolic appointee he wanted him to be sure that he understood that God was the Owner of the Church: "But if I tarry long, that thou mayest know how thou oughtest to behave thyself in the house of God, which is the church of the living God, the pillar and ground of the truth" (1 Tim. 3:15).

Christ is the head of the Church and Christians are the members of the body or body parts. These members are made up of people from all ages, languages, cultures, and nations. There are many members comprising one body. "So we, being many, are one body in Christ, and every one members one of another" (Rom. 12:5). There is one Church in the global sense, made up of those who have been saved and sanctified by Christ. "Husbands, love your wives, even as Christ also loved the church, and gave himself for it, that he might sanctify and cleanse it with the washing of water by the word; that he might present it to himself a glorious church, not having spot or wrinkle, or any such thing; but that it should be holy and without blemish" (Eph. 5:25–27). Local assemblies of diversified denominations dot the globe and make up the one Church. A person's denominational tag isn't worth a biscuit. I've heard it said that it will either fall off on the way to heaven or burn off on the way to hell. It will be of no value in either place. It is only by faith in Christ alone that the Holy Spirit places us in the body of Christ and secures us as a citizen of heaven. "For by one Spirit were we all baptized into one body, whether we be Jews or Greeks, whether we be bond or free; and have been all made to drink into one Spirit. For the body is not one member, but many" (1 Cor. 12:13–14)

LOCAL CHURCHES WORLDWIDE

There are local assemblies of believers in almost every corner of the world. They meet for corporate worship, praise, prayer, fellowship, preaching and teaching of God's Word. God has given certain ones among them special spiritual gifts for the perfecting of the saints and the work of the ministry. These leaders are responsible to administer many things, of which baptism and remembering the Lord table is especially important. It is an awesome responsibility to be an overseer of God's flock. Christ the good Shepherd has a special crown for those who do the job well. The Apostle Peter makes a clear charge to the leaders: "Feed the flock of God which is among you, taking the oversight of it, not by constraint but willingly; not for filthy lucre but of a ready mind; neither as being lords over God's heritage, but being examples to the flock. And when the chief Shepherd shall appear, ye shall receive a crown of glory that fadeth not away" (1 Pet. 5:2–4). The local church is a blessing. Believers do themselves a great favor when they actively participate with other believers on a weekly basis.

THE CHURCH TRIUMPHANT

The Church is to continue steadfastly in the Apostles' doctrine and in fellowship with one another: "And they continued steadfastly in the apostles' doctrine and fellowship, and in breaking of bread, and prayers" (Acts 2:42). This side of eternity the Church is given the responsibility to preach and teach the gospel and make disciples of all nations. We are to expect opposition to the task on all fronts; from within (our flesh), from without (worldly philosophies), and from the powers of darkness led by Satan himself. We needn't fear, for God has promised that the Church is guaranteed not to fail. Long after this old world has come and gone, the Church will continue its ministry of glorifying God. "To the praise of the glory of his grace, through which he hath made us accepted in the beloved" (Eph. 1:6). "And hath raised us up together, and made us sit together in heavenly places in Christ Jesus; that in the ages to come he might show the exceeding riches of his grace in his kindness toward us through Christ Jesus" (Eph. 2:6).

Oh, the victory of the cross and empty tomb! Oh, the fulfilled promise of the Holy Spirit's coming at Pentecost. The heavens will forever resound in triumphant praise. "After this I beheld and, lo, a great multitude, which no man could number, of all nations, and kindred's, and peoples, and tongues, stood before the throne, and before the Lamb, clothed with white robes, and palms in their hands, and cried with a loud voice, saying, Salvation to our God who sitteth upon the throne, and unto the Lamb. And all the angels stood round about the throne, and about the elders and the four living creatures, and fell before the throne on their faces, and worshiped God, saying, Amen! Blessing, and glory, and wisdom, and thanksgiving, and honor, and power, and might be unto our God forever and ever. Amen" (Rev. 7:9–12).

THE HARVEST

This Pentecost, or Feast of Harvest, of which we speak was accompanied by a great harvest of souls. Peter preached his first Holy Spirit-anointed sermon and about three thousand souls were born again. When Holy Spirit-anointed sermons are preached, you can anticipate a harvest of souls. No person has ever been born again without the preaching of the gospel and the work of the Holy Spirit. "Say not ye, There are yet four months, and then cometh harvest? Behold, I say unto you, Lift up your eyes, and look on the fields; for they are white already to harvest" (Jn. 4:35) When Jesus sent out the seventy to go and preach the gospel He said this to them:; "Therefore said he unto them, The harvest truly is great, but the laborers are few; pray ye, therefore the Lord of the harvest, that he would send forth laborers into his harvest" (Lk. 10:2). On that Feast of Pentecost there were people in Jerusalem who were ripe for the gospel and salvation. Even now there are people in our neighborhoods and towns who are also ripe for salvation. It is the same Holy Spirit of Pentecost who worked in their hearts then as it is who will work in their hearts now. It is the same gospel and the same Savior.

ONE ACCORD

The disciples were with one accord and in one place. This is no small statement but very essential for the coming and working of the Holy Spirit, both then and now. David understood the importance of unity and oneness among believers when he wrote, "Behold, how good and how pleasant it is for brethren to dwell together in unity! It is like the precious ointment upon the head, that ran down upon the beard, even Aaron's beard; that went down to the skirts of his garments, like the dew of Hermon, and like the dew that descended upon the mountains of Zion; for there the Lord commanded the blessings, even life for evermore" (Ps. 133:1–3). Oh how good and pleasant in the sight of God as well as in the sight of men. The disciples were not strangers to quarrelling and bickering. On the evening of the last supper they were debating over who would be top dog in the coming kingdom. "And there was also a strife among them, which of them should be accounted the greatest. And he said unto them, The kings of the Gentiles exercise lordship over them; and they that exercise authority upon them are called benefactors. But ye shall not be so; but he that is greatest among you, let him be as the younger; and he that is chief, as he that doth serve. For which is greater, he that dineth, or he that serveth? Is not he that dineth? But I am among you as he that serveth" (Lk. 22:24–27). After He said these things to them He got a towel and basin of water and washed their feet.

It was unthinkable that they would wash one another's feet; it was even more so that their Lord should wash their feet. They were going to need help if they were going to be in one accord when the Holy Spirit came.

BREATHE ON ME BREATH OF GOD

On Resurrection Day Jesus appeared to His disciples and showed Himself alive. Jesus knowing all men and knowing what was in them; including His disciples, knew they would need divine help if they were to be in one accord on Pentecost. He gave them, as it were, a preparatory portion of the Holy Spirit before the full endowment that would come in fifty days. There was one disciple who was absent, Thomas, more commonly referred to as doubting Thomas. We'll talk about him more in a minute. "Then said Jesus to them again, Peace be unto you; as my Father hath sent me, even so send I you. And when he had said this, he breathed on them, and saith unto them, Receive ye the Holy Spirit; whosoever's sins ye remit, they are remitted unto them; and whosoever's sins ye retain, they are retained" (Jn. 20:21–23). First, Jesus gave them their commission then He gave them what they needed most – the breath of the Holy Spirit. Breath is the most urgent need we have to sustain physical life. In the same way the Holy Spirit is the most urgent need we have to sustain spiritual life. The disciples could remit sins on terms of the gospel only and no other. "Whom God hath set forth to be a propitiation through faith in his blood, to declare his righteousness for the remission of sins that are past, through the forbearance of God" (Rom. 3:25).

Remember, Thomas wasn't present then. Later, he was foolishly bold in his unbelief. He crudely spoke of putting his fingers in the holes of Jesus' hands and thrusting his hand in

Jesus' side before he would believe. The following Sunday he was given the opportunity. For Christ Himself, Who through the eternal Spirit had offered Himself without spot to God came and purged Thomas' conscience from dead works so he could serve the living God. Thomas was instantly humbled and confessed Him as his Lord and his God. Jesus acknowledged his faith and now the whole group was in one accord.

Over the next days and weeks the disciples spent more time in prayer than usual. This is a great asset for any group of believers who desire unity of the Spirit among themselves. This was a season of yielding rights and self-denial, of putting one another before themselves. They were sensing the inner working of the Holy Spirit teaching them the blessing of being peacemakers. They were seeing the value of meekness and humility. A genuine love for one another was becoming evident as the Holy Spirit brought to their remembrance the words of Jesus. Words like "by this shall all men know that ye are my disciples if ye love one another." I believe the same power of the Holy Spirit that brought the disciples into one accord then is available for us Christians today. Paul encourages us with these words: "I therefore, the prisoner of the Lord, beseech you that ye walk worthy of the vocation to which ye are called, with all lowliness and meekness, with longsuffering, forbearing one another in love, endeavoring to keep the unity of the Spirit in the bond of peace" (Eph. 4:1–3). The unity of the Spirit is a powerful thing worth all the effort it takes to obtain.

OBEDIENCE AND PATIENCE

The disciples were instructed not to leave Jerusalem but to wait for the promise of the Father. Jerusalem, Jerusalem, the favored city of God. The city where the Lord Jesus was crucified and three days later rose from the dead. It was only fitting that Jerusalem would be the place where a new phase of God's revelation to man would begin. The Holy Spirit, Whose presence would enable the disciples to do greater works than Jesus did among them, would come to them in overwhelming power. "Verily, verily, I say unto you, He that believeth on me, the works that I do shall he do also; and greater works than these shall he do, because I go unto my Father" (Jn. 14:12). They were about to be baptized with the Holy Spirit. "For John truly baptized with water; but ye shall be baptized with the Holy Spirit not many days from now" (Acts 1:5). There is no indication in Scripture that the disciples knew the details in advance of what was about to occur. This would seem a good example to follow when waiting for the Holy Spirit to do a work of grace in our personal lives.

WHAT AN ENTRANCE

I love the word "suddenly". When the Holy Spirit came on the Feast of Pentecost, He didn't come gradually as they might have been expecting. We can note this about the Holy Spirit; His entrance was sudden. I recently prayed with a man who came forward, confessed his sin and put his faith in Christ as his Savior. I spoke with him a few moments later. He said he never expected this to happen to him. He grew up in a pastor's home. He had been in church all his life. He was a good guy. He considered himself a Christian, confident he was on his way to heaven. Then the light of the gospel busted into his life and he was suddenly broken before God. He responded in faith. The Apostle Paul's conversion was also a sudden unexpected event; "And as he journeyed, he came near Damascus, and suddenly there shone round about him a light from heaven" (Acts 9:3).

When the Holy Spirit came upon the disciples, there was a sound from heaven. The sound was from heaven, not from hell. It came from above and not from beneath. There is a distinct difference between the Holy Spirit and the spirit that works in the sons of darkness. This was unmistakably the promise for which they had been waiting. It was being fulfilled in the very house where they were sitting. The sound was like the sound of a mighty rushing wind and was in every corner of the house. The Holy Spirit filled the house of the occupants and the occupants of the house at the same time. "And they were all filled with the Holy Spirit" (Acts 2:4a)

THE WIND

Why the wind? Often times the Holy Spirit is likened to a wind or breath. There is no life without breath. The Holy Spirit was breathing spiritual life into the disciples in a fuller and more powerful way than they had ever experienced. God once showed Ezekiel a large valley full of dry bones and during the tour asked him if the bones could live. Ezekiel answered that he didn't know if they could or not but he knew God never asked a question without knowing the answer, so he said, "Lord God thou knowest." God then told Ezekiel to prophesy to the bones. While he prophesied God would bring them together and give them life. So Ezekiel preached to the dry bones and they came together. Sinew, flesh, and skin came upon the bones, but there was no breath in them. God commanded Ezekiel to prophecy to the wind and the bones would come to life. "Then said he unto me, Prophecy unto the wind, prophecy, son of man, and say to the wind, Thus saith the Lord God; Come from the four winds, O breath, and breathe upon these slain, that they may live. So

I prophesied as he commanded me, and the breath came into them, and they lived, and stood up upon their feet, an exceedingly great army" (Ezek. 37:9, 10). That prophecy may well have been fulfilled May 14th, 1948, when the Jewish people once again established Israel as their homeland. The point is, God's Spirit is likened to a powerful wind that gives life. I would never preach another sermon if I didn't have the expectant hope that the life-giving wind of the Holy Spirit might blow upon the listeners.

The wind which announced the coming of the Holy Spirit on Pentecost may well have shaken the house. Mighty winds have the ability to shake things up. Later, after the Sanhedrin threatened the Spirit-filled disciples not to preach any more in Jesus' Name, they continued to minister just the same. They gathered for prayer and this is what happened: "And when they had prayed, the place was shaken where they were assembled together; and they were all filled with the Holy Spirit, and they spoke the word of God with boldness" (Acts 4:31).

About 15 years ago, I was preaching in Anchorage, Alaska. We were staying with some church folks who had a very lovely home with a room for us on the second floor. About midnight we awoke to the sound of a powerful wind. The house shook for about an hour before it eventually calmed down. In the morning we looked around outside and saw shingles missing from most of the nearby homes. One neighbor was even missing a portion of his roof. We were told it was a Chinook wind that had reached gusts of nearly 100 mph.

The wind which announced the coming of the Holy Spirit on Pentecost was so noticeable that it caught the attention of the multitude in Jerusalem. The coming of the Lord Jesus as a babe was only witnessed by a handful of shepherds; even the inn keeper was oblivious to what was happening in his own stable. The lowly entrance of Christ was all part of God's plan. But rest assured He will make up for it in His second coming. He will come in the clouds with power and great glory.

Cloven Tongues of Fire

John the Baptist made a distinction between his baptism with water and the baptism of Christ with fire. "I, indeed, baptize you with water unto repentance, but he who cometh after me is mightier than I, whose shoes I am not worthy to bear; he shall baptize you with the Holy Spirit, and with fire" (Mt. 3:11). It's important to note that the cloven tongues of fire appeared upon each of them individually. They could see it alight upon everyone but themselves. I wonder if Spirit-filled people are more likely to see the work of God evident in others before they see it in themselves.

Why fire? When fire is harnessed it translates into power. If the spark plugs are firing, the motor vehicle can travel and even haul a load. "But ye shall receive power, after the Holy Spirit is come upon you; and ye shall be witnesses unto me both in Jerusalem, and in all Judea, and in Samaria, and unto the uttermost part of the earth" (Acts 1:8). The indwelling presence of the Holy Spirit is the power of God for us to carry out the ministry of His commission and help us live a sanctified life. It is impossible for a Christian to purify his soul in the energy of the flesh. "Elect according to the foreknowledge of God, the Father, through sanctification of the Spirit, unto obedience and the sprinkling of the blood of Jesus Christ; Grace unto you, and peace, be multiplied" (1 Pet. 1:2). We can only purify our souls through the sanctifying power of the Holy Spirit.

FILLED WITH THE HOLY SPIRIT

When the Holy Spirit came on Pentecost, the disciples were baptized with the Holy Spirit. This event marked the birth of the Church. Now, as members are added to the Church by faith in Christ, the Holy Spirit baptizes them into the body of Christ as well: "For by one Spirit were we baptized into one body, whether we be Jews or Greeks, whether we be bond or free; and have been all made to drink into one Spirit" (1 Cor. 12:13). The disciples were baptized with the Holy Spirit and at the same time they were filled with the Holy Spirit. There is one baptism and many fillings. "One Lord, one faith, one baptism" (Eph. 4:5). As the Church grew and became more established in the faith they were instructed to be filled with the Spirit. "And be not drunk with wine, in which is excess, but be filled with the Spirit" (Eph. 5:18). Pentecost is a glorious picture of both the baptism and a filling happening simultaneously.

The Holy Spirit had been poured out upon them in such a way that they began experiencing a variety of joys and wisdom they had never known before. Their love for God was overflowing and they had to speak to others of His goodness. They had a greater power for ministry than they had ever known. They received divine gifts that would enable them to obey the commission given to them by Christ. As men filled with wine lose inhibitions and do things that make them look like fools, so the filling of the Holy Spirit caused them to lose foolish inhibitions that kept them from identifying with Christ. Pentecost marked the beginning of a new day, a new potential for men and women of all ages and from every country under heaven to personally experience the joys of knowing and serving God.

THEY SPOKE WITH OTHER TONGUES

"And they were all filled with the Holy Spirit, and began to speak with other tongues, as the Spirit gave them utterance" Acts 2:4). The Greek word for tongues is glossa and here refers to languages. Jerusalem was filled with pilgrims from many different countries who spoke many different languages. The Holy Spirit supernaturally gifted the disciples to speak languages they had never learned. The disciples spoke Hebrew with an obvious Galilean accent yet now they were able to speak other languages fluently. "And there were dwelling at Jerusalem Jews, devout men, out of every nation under heaven. Now when this was noised abroad, the multitude came together, and were confounded, because every man heard them speak in his own language. And they were all amazed and marveled, saying one to another, Behold, are not all these who speak Galileans? And how here we every man in his own tongue, wherein he was born?" (Acts 2:5–8). In the following verses it lists some 15 different nations and dialects. The languages were different but the message was the same: they were all declaring the wonderful works of God.

BLASPHEMOUS UNBELIEF

The sin of unbelief always makes fools of us but to attribute the works of the Holy Spirit to something as low as drunkenness is unbelief at its worst. "Others, mocking, said, These men are full of new wine" (Acts 2:13). Since when does getting drunk enable a person to speak fluently a foreign language they had never learned? I have chosen to be a teetotaler, but I would be tempted to drink a six pack if I knew I could speak fluent French or German or Spanish or Chinese in one easy lesson. Even Rosetta Stone® can't boast those kinds of results. "Be not deceived, God is not mocked, for whatever a man soweth, that shall he also reap" (Gal. 6:7). If we sow unbelief to the things of the Spirit we shouldn't expect to harvest the blessings of faith.

PETER'S GREAT SERMON

Peter stood up and told the people they were not drunk. He asked them to listen. His text was Joel 2:28–32. After quoting his text he preached the greatness of Christ. He told them of God's plan of redemption. He concluded his sermon with these words: "Therefore, let all the house of Israel know assuredly, that God hath made this same Jesus, whom ye have crucified, both Lord and Christ" (Acts 2:36). The Holy Spirit took his sermon and did the work of revelation and conviction. Many of them realize they needed to do something with what they had heard. "Now when they had heard this, they were pricked in their heart, and said unto Peter and to the rest of the apostles, Men and brethren, what shall we do?" (Acts 2:37). Oh that we might learn from Peter's example. There was no quenching of the Spirit here; without hesitation he gave them instruction: "Then Peter said unto them, Repent, and be baptized, every one of you, in the name of Jesus Christ for the remission of sins, and ye shall receive the gift of the Holy Spirit" (Acts 2:38). Being filled with the Holy Spirit he was led to give further exhortation and admonition. "For the promise is unto you, and to your children, and to all that are afar off, even as many as the Lord, our God, shall call. And with many other words did he testify and exhort, saying, Save yourselves from this crooked generation" (Acts 2:39–40).

The greatness of Peter's sermon lay not in his text or the style of his delivery but in the fact that he was a man filled with the Holy Spirit. Peter and the early Church had a lot to learn about the Spirit-filled life but they were on their way and they knew God would be faithful to teach them. In some ways it was like when Jesus was with them in person, but in other ways it seemed their relationship with God was even more personal. Their walk with the Lord always required faith but faith would be more important now. They would have to listen to His voice and develop ears to hear what the Spirit would say to them. I believe they were excited at this new venture of faith, but I also believe they were somewhat anxious and concerned about the unknown. As their questions arose, I believe the peace that Jesus gave them bore witness with their spirits and they knew it was going to be okay. The fruit of the Spirit from Galatians 5:22&23 would become the signature of the Spirit-filled life.

CHAPTER FOUR

THE SPIRIT'S WITNESS IN SALVATION

Salvation is a spiritual experience and cannot occur without the work of the Holy Spirit. The Holy Spirit is responsible for bringing about genuine conviction of sin. He reproves the sinner of his unbelief and enables him to have faith in the gospel of Christ. Without the work of the Holy Spirit it is impossible for a man to see the worthlessness of his self-righteousness. God's standard of righteousness is beyond man's ability to attain apart from the grace of God in Christ Jesus. The Holy Spirit ministers that grace resulting in a fear of the judgment to come. Fear of coming judgment is a kindness of the Holy Spirit and one of the great incentives for man not to neglect so great salvation. "And when he is come, he will reprove the world of sin, and of righteousness, and of judgment: Of sin, because they believe not on me; Of righteousness, because I go to my Father, and ye see me no more; Of judgment, because the prince of this world is judged" (Jn. 16:8–11). Without the work of the Holy Spirit a person cannot be born again. "That which is born of the flesh is flesh; and that which is born of the Spirit is spirit" (Jn. 3:6).

THE HOLY SPIRIT AND MAN

At this point I believe it would be helpful to note some general truths regarding the inner workings of the Holy Spirit and man. For example: The Holy Spirit can be lied to. He cannot be deceived, but He can be lied to. Deception can only occur when you believe a lie and God never believes a lie. In the early church a husband and wife tried to look better before the church than they really were. They came across like they were giving their all when in fact they were keeping back some for themselves. "But a certain man named Ananias, with Sapphira, his wife, sold a possession, and kept back part of the price, his wife also knowing of it, and brought a certain part, and laid it at the apostles' feet. But Peter said, Ananias, why hath Satan filled thine heart to lie to the Holy Spirit, and to keep back part of the price of the land? While it remained, was it not thine own? And after it sold, was it not in thine own power? Why hast thou conceived this thing in thine heart? Thou hast not lied unto men, but unto God" (Acts 5:1–4).

The Holy Spirit can be grieved. He feels sorrow or pain of heart when people pursue destructive behavior that so often results in harmful consequences. As a child I did some things that grieved my parents. As I look back on it now I know their grief was evidence of their love for me. They wanted the best for me. This short verse speaks volumes about the love of God and His genuine care for our best interest: "And grieve not the Holy Spirit of God, by whom ye are sealed unto the day of redemption" (Eph. 4:30).

The Holy Spirit can be quenched. "Quench not the Spirit" (1 Th. 5:19). To quench means to snuff out or extinguish, to stifle. We are baptized with the Holy Spirit and with fire. He works as a refining fire, by enlightening and purifying our souls. We must be careful not to quench this holy fire which is so necessary for His sanctifying work in us. Fire can be extinguished by water or dirt so we must be careful not to indulge in carnal lusts or to mind earthly things. More will be said in our next chapter on the Spirit's witness in sanctification.

The Holy Spirit can be resisted. Stephen was a man full of faith and the Holy Spirit. He preached a Holy Spirit-anointed sermon filled with scripture. His listeners, however, chose to resist the Holy Spirit even though they were cut to the heart; "Ye stiff-necked and uncircumcised in heart and ears, ye do always resist the Holy Spirit; as your fathers did, so do ye" (Acts 7:51). A stiffed neck is the same thing as a hard heart, one that remains closed. A tender heart, though, is receptive to the things of God. A tender heart resists the devil, but hard hearts resist God.

The Holy Spirit can be blasphemed. "Wherefore, I say unto you, All manner of sin and blasphemy shall be forgiven men; but the blasphemy against the Holy Spirit shall not be forgiven men. And whosoever speaketh a word against the Son of man, it shall be forgiven him; but whosoever speaketh against the Holy Spirit, it shall not be forgiven him, neither in this age, neither in the age to come" (Mt. 12:31–32). The tongue has great capacity for speaking good or evil and here it is credited for a sin that is unpardonable. This most serious sin of the Pharisees was their continual denial of the obvious truth that the miracles of Jesus were done by the power of God. The sin of unbelief keeps a person in a state of condemnation where the act of faith would receive forgiveness from God and become a partaker of the heavenly gift of salvation. The unpardonable sin is the sin of not believing God's Word is true.

OUR BODY HIS TEMPLE

The Holy Spirit does not live in a temple made with hands; neither is He worshiped with men's hands but He lives in the bodies of born-again believers. "What? Know ye not that your body is the temple of the Holy Spirit who is in you, whom ye have of God, and ye are not your own?" (1 Cor. 6:19). The Holy Spirit does many things in the life of a believer but most of what He does falls under the canopy of bearing witness with our spirit that we are the children of God. The workings of the Holy Spirit in the inner man are the best evidence of a person's salvation.

HE IS OUR TEACHER

As children of God we have many things to learn. It is impossible to learn them without the help of the Holy Spirit. Jesus said He had many things to say to His disciples but they were not able to bear them. In due time the Holy Spirit would reveal these things as they became able to understand them. "But the anointing which ye have received of him abideth in you, and ye need not that any man teach you; but as the same anointing teacheth you of all things, and is truth, and is no lie, and even as it hath taught you, ye shall abide in him" (1 Jn. 2:27). This does not mean that we throw spiritual teachers to the wind for God has given to the Church pastor-teachers who labor and study diligently to help us grow.

As we grow on in our walk with the Lord He reveals deep things, things that are hidden from those who do not have the Spirit of God. Many of the moral principles and religious teachings of the Bible are within the capacity of the unsaved man to understand. It is the divine unfolding and revelation of the gospel of redemption that is impossible to grasp without the Holy Spirit. The doctrines of sin and grace, mercy and hope, faith and eternity, love and fear of judgment, are the things impossible to comprehend without the revealing work of the Holy Spirit. "But God hath revealed them unto us by his Spirit; for the Spirit searcheth all things, yea, the deep things of God. For what man knoweth the things of a man, except the spirit of man which is in him? Even so the things of God knoweth no man, but the Spirit of God. Now we have received, not the spirit of the world, but the Spirit who is of God; that we might know the things that are freely given to us of God. Which things also we speak, not in the words which man's wisdom teacheth, but which the Holy Spirit teacheth, comparing spiritual things with spiritual" (1 Cor. 2:9–13).

It is also the work of the Holy Spirit to reveal new depths to old truths, keeping us ever in awe of the depth and greatness of God and His Word. On our best day we would never be sharp enough to figure out the spiritual truths of God's word on our own. David said; "Show me thy ways, O Lord; teach me thy paths. Lead me in thy truth, and teach me; for thou art the God of my salvation; on thee do I wait all the day" (Ps. 25:4–5). When a person comes to the Scriptures as a know-it-all, he will be left to his own devices. But when a person comes with a teachable spirit, the Lord delights to teach him. "In that hour Jesus rejoiced in the Spirit, and said, I thank thee, O Father, Lord of heaven and earth, that thou hast hidden these things from the wise and prudent, and hast revealed them unto babes. Even so, Father; for so it seemed good in thy sight" (Lk. 10:21).

He Comforts, Counsels and Guides

"And I will pray the Father, and he shall give you another Comforter, that he may abide with you forever; even the Spirit of truth, whom the world cannot receive, because it seeth him not, neither knoweth him: but ye know him; for he dwelleth with you, and shall be in you. I will not leave you comfortless; I will come to you" (Jn. 14:16–18). The Greek word for comforter is parakletos meaning "one who is called alongside to help"; thus, a counselor. When life presents us with difficulties that have the capacity to unravel the very fiber of our being, many times the Holy Spirit provides counsel and comfort we could never have manufactured in our own strength. He guides us in the way of truth and leads us in the way everlasting. Often time temporal values consume our time and energy, the things of eternal value are ignored to meet present demands. "Search me, O God, and know my heart; try me, and know my thoughts; and see if there be any wicked way in me, and lead me in the way everlasting" (Ps. 139:23–24). It is the Holy Spirit who counsels and guides us to lay up treasures in heaven that can't be devalued or taken away. Oh the blessed ministry of the Holy Spirit that bears witness that we are children of God.

He Calls Ministers and Sends Out Workers

The Apostle Paul was called to minister as an apostle. "Paul, a servant of Jesus Christ, called to be an apostle, separated unto the gospel of God" (Rom. 1:1). He was thankful for the ministry God had given him. "And I thank Christ Jesus, our Lord, who hath enabled me, in that he counted me faithful, putting me into the ministry" (1 Tim 1:12). Paul and Barnabas were thriving in their ministry at Antioch when the Holy Spirit called and sent them out as the first foreign missionaries. "As they ministered to the Lord, and fasted, the Holy Spirit said, Separate me Barnabas and Saul for the work unto which I have called them. And when they had fasted and prayed, and laid their hands on them, they sent them away. So they, being sent forth by the Holy Spirit, departed unto Seleucia; and from there they sailed to Cyprus" (Acts 13:2–4). It is a powerful affirmation of salvation to sense a call from God in the gospel ministry.

HE GIVES SPIRITUAL GIFTS AND POWER

"Now there are diversities of gifts, but the same Spirit. And there are differences of administrations, but the same Lord. And there are diversities of operations, but it is the same God who worketh all in all. But the manifestation of the Spirit is given to every man to profit. For one is given, by the Sprit, the word of wisdom; to another, the word of knowledge by the same Spirit; to another, faith by the same Spirit, to another, the gifts of healing by the same Spirit; to another, the working of miracles; to another, prophecy, to another, discerning of spirits; to another, various kinds of tongues; to another, the interpretation of tongues. But all these worketh that one and the very same Spirit, dividing to every man severally as he will" (1 Cor. 12:4–11). There is no room for self-choosing in regard to spiritual gifts. Every believer receives a spiritual gift, no one is left out. Though the gifts are diverse, they are all honorable and necessary for the work of the ministry in the body of Christ.

The Apostle Paul was regularly exhorting believers to be steadfast in their faith and walk in the ways of the Lord. More than likely his spiritual gift was exhortation. In his Romans 12 list of gifts he gives instructions on the use and care of spiritual gifts; "Having then gifts differing according to the grace that is given to us, whether prophecy, let us prophesy according to the proportion of faith; or ministry, let us wait on our ministering; or he that teacheth, on teaching; or he that exhorteth, on exhortation; he that giveth, let him do it with liberality; he that ruleth, with diligence; he that showeth mercy, with cheerfulness" (Rom. 12:6–8). Paul knew of the divine enabling power of God in the use of spiritual gifts and testified of it in his letter to the church at Corinth. "And I was with you in weakness, and in fear, and in much trembling. And my speech and preaching were not with enticing words of man's wisdom, but in demonstration of the Spirit and of power; that your faith should not stand in the wisdom of men, but in the power of God" (1 Cor. 2:3–5). The Holy Spirit gives gifts to men. He is also the power behind those gifts.

HE WARNS AND RESTRAINS

We are commanded to walk in the Spirit. "This I say then, Walk in the Spirit, and ye shall not fulfill the lust of the flesh" (Gal. 5:16). Walking is our most common mode of travel. Paul uses it frequently to describe the lifestyle of the spiritual Christian. According to John 16:13, the Holy Spirit will show us things to come. I believe He does so as we walk with Him. I have heard people say many times, I am glad I don't know the future. The Holy Spirit knows the future and can lead us around dangers that could be avoided if we have spiritual ears. I believe the Spirit can bear witness with my spirit and tell me not to take a certain route, engage in a certain conversation or volunteer involvement in a certain activity. I believe He can prompt me to share a word or kind deed for a specific purpose. This is more subjective than some people care to go in their walk, but nonetheless I believe it is part of the witness of His Spirit. "For as many as are led by the Spirit of God, they are the sons of God" (Rom. 8:14).

In Paul's second missionary journey he was desirous of preaching the gospel in many places of Asia. The Holy Spirit restrained him. He made several attempts to go to other places but the Holy Spirit didn't let him. Then, he was given a vision of a man in Macedonia begging him to come over and help them. He took it from the Lord and set his course for Macedonia; "Now when they had gone throughout Phrygia and the region of Galatia, and were forbidden by the Holy Spirit to preach the word in Asia, after they were come to Mysia, they attempted to go into Bithynia; but the Spirit allowed them not. And they passing by Mysia, came down to Troas. And a vision appeared to Paul in the night: there stood a man of Macedonia, beseeching him, and saying, Come over into Macedonia, and help us" (Acts 16:6–9). Every well-meaning Christian who wants to serve the Lord would do well to respect both the red and green lights of the Holy Spirit.

HE BEARS FRUIT AND GLORIFIES JESUS

"But the fruit of the Spirit is love, joy, peace, long-suffering, gentleness, goodness, faith, meekness, self-control; against such there is no law" (Gal. 5:22–23). The fruit of the Spirit, in whomsoever they are found, plainly show they are led by the Spirit. It reveals they are no longer under the Law but under grace. Grace is the power of God, not to just cease doing evil, but to do good, to be about the business of glorifying Christ. "[The Spirit of truth] shall glorify me; for he shall receive of mine, and shall show it unto you" (Jn. 16:14). We know we are glorifying Christ when we grow strong in grace and see the fruit of the Spirit being supernaturally produced in our life.

Let's consider love, joy and peace. I suggest the best way to measure your theology is by your love for God with all your heart, mind, soul, and strength. The best way to measure your love for God is by your love for people. "If a man says, I love

God, and hateth his brother, he is a liar; for he that loveth not his brother, whom he hath seen, how can he love God, whom he hath not seen? And this commandment have we from him, that he who loveth God love his brother also" (1 Jn. 4:20–21). Jesus never loved us because we were so loveable; "But God commendeth his love toward us in that, while we were yet sinners, Christ died for us" (Rom. 5:8).

Joy is inseparably related to our salvation. Our salvation cannot be taken away from us. So we should never let anyone steal our joy. "Behold, God is my salvation; I will trust, and not be afraid; for the Lord, even the Lord, is my strength and my song; he also is become my salvation. Therefore, with joy shall ye draw water out of the wells of salvation" (Isa. 12:2–3). The Holy Spirit Himself is a wellspring of life springing up into everlasting life. In the midst of absolute economic disaster the prophet Habakkuk experiences supernatural joy related to his salvation: "Yet I will rejoice in the Lord, I will joy in the God of my salvation" (Hab. 3:18).

What about supernatural peace? Man-made peace always deteriorates but the peace of God sustains us. "And the peace of God, which passeth all understanding, shall keep your hearts and minds through Christ Jesus" (Phil. 4:7). "Therefore, being justified by faith, we have peace with God through our Lord Jesus Christ" (Rom. 5:1).

SELF EXAMINATION

We have discussed many of the ministries of the Holy Spirit. Though not an exhaustive list, they are some of the ways the Spirit bears witness with our spirit that we are children of God. If a person believes himself to be born again and yet has no desire for the things of the Spirit of God and no evidence of spiritual fruit, he may want to consider Paul's exhortation to do a self-examination. "Examine yourselves, whether you are in the faith; prove yourselves. Know ye not yourselves how Jesus Christ is in you, unless you are discredited?" (2Cor. 13:5) The one exam you don't want to fail is the one concerning the faith. Don't examine your faith for it will always come up short. A weak faith can save you, a weak Savior cannot. Ask the Holy Spirit to help you in your exam. Study the faith. "As ye have, therefore, received Christ Jesus the Lord, so walk ye in him, rooted and built up in him, and established in 'the faith', as ye have been taught, abounding in thanksgiving" (Col. 2:6–7). I'll close this chapter with a favorite encouragement to my own soul; "Beloved, when I gave all diligence to write unto you of the common salvation, it was needful for me to write unto you, and exhort you that you should earnestly contend for 'the faith' which was once delivered unto the saints" (Jude 3). Your faith is more likely to prosper the deeper it is rooted in the faith. I can give no greater instruction for the doubting saint than to get a grip on the Gospel. If you are saved, the Gospel will get a grip on you and the Spirit will bear witness that you are His. The Holy Spirit's ministry is to bear witness with our spirit that we are the children of God.

THE SPIRIT'S WITNESS IN SANCTIFICATION

One of the greatest assurances of salvation is the Holy Spirit's witness in progressive sanctification as we grow in the grace and knowledge of our Lord and Savior Jesus Christ. In justification we are recipients only. God declares us holy and righteous by our faith in the merits of Christ's sinless life and His sacrificial death on the cross alone. When Jesus said, "It is finished", the penalty of sin was paid and the justice of God was satisfied. Positionally we are complete. Nothing more need be or could be done to make us any more right with God. "And ye are complete in him, who is the head of all principality and power" (Col. 2:10). God accepts us on the basis of faith alone in Christ alone. "To the praise of the glory of his grace, through which he hath made us accepted in the beloved" (Eph. 1:6). We are also positionally sanctified, declared holy: "And such were some of you; but ye are washed, but ye are sanctified, but ye are justified in the name of the Lord Jesus, and by the Spirit of our God" (1Cor. 6:11).

Progressive sanctification is something we are participants

in. It is bringing our behavior in line with our identity. Our faith becomes stronger and increases as we learn to walk in obedience to the will and ways of God found in His Word. In Jesus' prayer for His disciples He made His desire clear: "Sanctify them through thy truth; thy word is truth" (Jn. 17:17). One of the main goals of Scripture is to establish us in the truth. not just a head knowledge of clinical facts about Scripture but the life transforming walk of a Holy Spirit-empowered follower of Jesus. Jesus sanctified Himself so we could have an example to follow. "And for their sakes I sanctify myself, that they also might be sanctified through the truth" (Jn. 17:19). Jesus was obedient to His father. He didn't come to do His own will but the will of the Father that sent Him. As we learn to walk in obedience to God's Word our relationship with Him is made more precious. We draw near to God and He draws near to us. We learn obedience is possible with the help of His Spirit. Though there are some costs, the benefits far outweigh them.

A good parent does not leave their child to raise himself but teaches him the way in which he should go. In concern for his safety, the child is given guidelines and rules that will help protect him from danger or accident. The parent helps the child learn obedience and makes it as easy as possible for him. In the same way the Holy Spirit is our Helper in learning obedience to God's commands. A relationship of love, trust, and respect develop and many hardships are avoided. The lifelong process of progressive sanctification is the way God shows His gracious loving care for His children. "For this is the love of God, that we keep his commandments: and his commandments are not burdensome" (1Jn 5:3).

The Importance of the Heart

The heart of the matter always seems to be the matter of the heart. The heart is the centermost part of our being which includes our intellect, emotions, and will. Jesus said where your treasure is, there will your heart be also. Sanctification must involve the heart. Over the years of my journey, purity of heart has eluded me on many occasions. Quite frankly, it's discouraging at times to realize the things that still live in the dim regions of my darkened heart, but bless God, it's in realizing His Spirit's witness in sanctification that I press on and grow stronger in my faith in Christ.

Peter wrote giving instructions on how to live Godly in the home and in the Church. His hope was that it would carry over into all human relationships. "But sanctify the Lord God in your hearts, and be ready always to give an answer to every man that asketh you a reason of the hope that is in you, with meekness and fear" (1 Pet. 3:15). To sanctify is to set apart the Lord as being first place in your heart. It is a commitment to serving and obeying Jesus as Lord of your life. It involves purifying your soul from sinful contaminants that hinder your walk with the Lord. It involves putting off the old man and his ways while putting on the new man which is created to be like Jesus. If I say that I love God, then it must evidence itself in a love for people. Peter raised the bar even higher when he said you must do it from the heart fervently. "Seeing that ye have purified your souls in obeying the truth through the Spirit unto unfeigned love of the brethren, see that you love one another with a pure heart fervently" (1 Pet. 1:22). I've been a Christian long enough to know, that at times some of the brethren aren't all that easy to love. As a matter of fact, at times they aren't even easy to like. The command though is all too clear: "Beloved, let us love one another; for love is of God, and everyone that loveth is born of God, and knoweth God. He that loveth not knoweth not God; for God is love. In this was manifested the love of God toward us, that God sent his only begotten Son into the world, that we might live through him. Herein is love, not that we loved God, but that he loved us, and sent his Son, to be the propitiation for our sins. Beloved, if God so loved us, we ought also to love one another. No man hath seen God at any time. If we love one another, God dwelleth in us, and his love is perfected in us. By this know we that we dwell in him, and he in us, because he hath given us of his Spirit" (1Jn 4:7–13) How can I do the seemingly impossible? How can I love someone I don't even like? "Because he hath given us of his Spirit". The important word here is of... Of is a preposition meaning 'to proceed from a source'. God the Holy Spirit is the Source of our strength. He enables us to do all things through Christ who strengthens us. Just as the Holy Spirit was the Source of Samson's physical strength in the Old Testament, so the Holy Spirit is the source of our spiritual strength in the New Testament.

SANCTIFICATION OF THE SPIRIT

Peter is referred to as the Apostle of hope. He is a seasoned follower of Christ and when under the inspiration of the Holy Spirit, he picks up the pen to write. It has been a long journey for him with many setbacks; lessons that took a long time in learning. In the introduction to his first letter he cuts right to the chase and he makes reference to the Trinity and their specific roles: "Elect according to the foreknowledge of God, the Father, through sanctification of the Spirit, unto obedience, and sprinkling of the blood of Jesus Christ: Grace unto you, and peace, be multiplied" (1Pet. 1:2). As we will see, this thing called sanctification through the Spirit unto obedience does not occur, as they say in a song and a prayer, but in many songs and many prayers.

BECOMING A PARTAKER OF THE DIVINE NATURE

My theology will never leave the printed page and translate into lifestyle without the following understanding of progressive sanctification. I will never experience divine power or what it means to become a partaker of the divine nature apart from the work of the Holy Spirit. I will be left to the power of the flesh and at best be only a spectator of the divine nature, not a participant. Grace and peace can only be multiplied through this knowledge of God and of the Lord Jesus. "According as his divine power hath given unto us all things that pertain unto life and godliness, through the knowledge of him that hath called us to glory and virtue; by which are given unto us exceedingly great and precious promises, that by these ye might be partakers of the divine nature, having escaped the corruption that is in the world through lust. And beside this, giving all diligence, add to your faith virtue; and to virtue, knowledge; and to knowledge, self-control; and to self-control, patience; and to patience, godliness; and to godliness, brotherly kindness; and to brotherly kindness, love. For if these things be in you, and abound, they make you that ye shall neither be barren nor unfruitful in the knowledge of our Lord Jesus Christ. But he that lacketh these things is blind and cannot see afar off, and hath forgotten that he was purged from his old sins. Wherefore the rather, brethren, give diligence to make your calling and election sure; for if ye do these things, ye shall never fall. For so an entrance shall be ministered unto you abundantly into the everlasting kingdom of our Lord and Savior, Jesus Christ" (2Pet.1:3–11)

ALL THINGS

Everything I need for life and godliness is found within the pages of God's Word. When a person receives Christ as Savior they do so in response to God's Word and God's Spirit. Both the Word of God and the God of the Word are involved. It is possible to hear God's Word and His Spirit but yet reject the offer of salvation. The "all things" promised by God in 2 Peter are only made available to those who by faith embrace them. "That by these [promises] ye might become partakers". "These promises" are here and now, "might become" is future tense, thus the process of progressive sanctification. There are many promises in God's Word. Here are two examples that have become especially precious to me: "I will not leave you comfortless; I will come to you" (Jn. 14:18). "And this is life eternal, that they might know thee, the only true God, and Jesus Christ, whom thou hast sent" (Jn. 17:3).

SPIRITUAL THINGS

In the Apostle Paul's letter to the church of Rome he makes reference to the things of the Spirit and the things of the flesh. He warns of the danger, the consequences, of being carnally minded. He also speaks of the blessings of being spiritually minded. "For they that are after the flesh do mind the things of the flesh; but they that are after the Spirit, the things of the Spirit. For to be carnally minded is death, but to be spiritually minded is life and peace" (Rom.8:5–6). Paul gives the same admonition in other letters also. "If ye, then, be risen with Christ, seek those things which are above, where Christ sitteth on the right hand of God. Set your affection on things above, not on things of the earth" (Col.3:1–2).

A short list of spiritual things would look something like this:

✧ private prayer
✧ singing unto the Lord
✧ reading and meditating on His Word
✧ private and corporate worship
✧ assembling with other believers for preaching and teaching
✧ thankfulness to God and others
✧ giving of your time, talent, and resources to help those in need
✧ missionary work
✧ humbleness of mind, a kind word, a caring look, a listening ear
✧ walking in the Spirit
✧ mortifying the deeds of the flesh
✧ evangelism
✧ forgiveness
✧ tender mercies, compassion, longsuffering, and joy

Paul gives a short list of fleshly things near the end of his first epistle. "Now the works of the flesh are manifest, which are these; adultery, fornication, uncleanness, lasciviousness, idolatry, sorcery, hatred, strife, jealousy, wrath, factions, seditions, heresies, envyings, murders, drunkenness, revelings, and the like" (Gal. 5:19–21a). The list could go on to include things like temporal values, bitterness, revenge, greed, self-righteousness, self-centeredness, and self-obsessions of all sorts.

The new man is characterized by the things of the Spirit, and the old man is characterized by the things of the flesh. We are instructed to put off the old man with his deeds and put on the new man. "Lie not one to another, seeing that ye have put off the old man with his deeds, and have put on the new man, that is renewed in knowledge after the image of him that created him" (Col.3:9–10). The new nature is opposed to the old nature and everything it represents. The old nature still wants to control the behavior of the child of God and the battle is on, big time! It is one thing to say, "Walk in the Spirit and you won't fulfill the lust of the flesh", it's another thing to do it. "For the flesh lusteth against the Spirit, and the Spirit against the flesh; and these are contrary the one to the other, so that ye cannot do the things that ye would. But if ye be led by the Spirit, ye are not under the law" (Gal 5:17–18).

SPIRITUAL DISCIPLINES

At the Great Commission the disciples were told to teach all nations the gospel and baptize them. They were instructed to teach the believers to observe all things they had been taught. In essence they were to make disciples. A disciple is a disciplined follower of Christ; one committed to the ways of the Lord. Disciples are not born, they are made. The spiritual disciplines, discipline in doing the spiritual things, are part of that process. Spiritual disciplines won't make you spiritual, but they will make you accessible to the Spirit of God Who in turn makes you spiritual. "Wherefore, my beloved, as ye have always obeyed, not as in my presence only but now much more in my absence, work out your own salvation with fear and trembling. For it is God who worketh in you both to will and to do of his good pleasure" (Phil. 2:12–13). God never intended for me to perform the spiritual life in the energy of the flesh as though it were something within the realm of my own power. I need help, the help that comes from on high. The spiritual disciplines, through the power of the Spirit, lead to a relationship with God, not just some meaningless performance of religious duties. "But if the Spirit of him that raised up Jesus from the dead dwell in you, he that raised up Christ from the dead shall also give life to your mortal bodies by his Spirit that dwelleth in you. Therefore, brethren, we are debtors, not to the flesh, to live after the flesh. For if ye live after the flesh, ye shall die; but if ye, through the Spirit, do mortify the deeds of the body, ye shall live. For as many as are led by the Spirit of God, they are the sons of God. For ye have not received the spirit of bondage again to fear; but ye have received the Spirit of adoption, whereby we cry, Abba, Father. The Spirit himself beareth witness with our spirit, that we are the children of God; and if children, then heirs – heirs of God, and joint heirs with Christ—if so be that we suffer with him, that we may be also glorified together. For I reckon that the sufferings of this present time are not worthy to be compared with the glory which shall be revealed in us" (Rom. 8:11–18). The Spirit Himself bears witness in my journey of faith, helping me, comforting me, and affirming that I am His child. He is my Father and I am His son.

SOWING AND REAPING

At the conclusion of Paul's letter to the churches of Galatia he gives them a simple but profound approach to going the distance in being a disciple of Christ. He has just encouraged them to walk in the Spirit. He has just made special reference to those who are spiritual. "Brethren, if a man be overtaken in a fault, ye who are spiritual restore such an one in the spirit of meekness, considering thyself, lest thou also be tempted" (Gal. 6:1). I don't know if we have a definition of one who is spiritual, but I like to think it's someone who is batting over 500, the Spirit over the flesh. I also think it is someone who, knowing his own propensity to failure, is meek in dealing with the failures of others. So within this context he sets forth this powerful truth which is so liberating if embraced. "Be not deceived, God is not mocked, for whatever a man soweth, that shall he also reap. For he that soweth to his flesh shall of the flesh reap corruption; but he that soweth to the Spirit shall of the Spirit reap life everlasting. And let us not be weary in well doing; for in due season we shall reap, if we faint not" (Gal.6:7–9).

Paul is not teaching a lesson on gardening, but he is taking the natural law of sowing and reaping and applying it to the spiritual life. If you sow corn you expect to harvest corn. If you plant potatoes you don't expect to dig tomatoes. You don't expect to go out to your apple tree and pick oranges. This law was established in Genesis 1:11–12 and it hasn't changed.

SOWING TO THE FLESH

Every day we sow seeds, either to the flesh or to the Spirit. Two important thoughts to consider before we go on is: (1) we harvest in a different season than we sow. Seeds don't produce a mature crop overnight. There is a season for every purpose under heaven.; and (2) sometimes the harvest is plentiful and sometimes it's lean. It is God Who gives the increase.

So what are some fleshly seeds?

Don't sow to covetousness. Sowing to covetousness means you treat people like things and things like people. "And he said unto them, Take heed, and beware of covetousness; for a man's life consisteth not in the abundance of the things which he possesseth" (Lk. 12:15). You may accumulate all the gadgets this world has to offer but you will reap a crop of loneliness with no U-Haul behind your hearse . . .

Don't sow to immorality. "For this is the will of God, even your sanctification, that ye should abstain from fornication" (1Th. 4:3). This sin can occur quite easily in our thoughts. Sow a thought, reap a deed; sow a deed, reap a habit; sow a habit, reap a character; sow a character, reap a destiny. The carnage of immorality is all too evident: regret, shame, pain, bondage, even perversion.

Don't sow to unforgiveness. "And be ye kind one to another, tenderhearted, forgiving one another, even as God, for Christ's sake, hath forgiven you" (Eph. 4:32). It's been said the only thing harder than forgiveness is unforgiveness. The unforgiving soul reaps a crop of suspicion, turmoil, conflict, revenge, and often mental illness. It produces bitterness which is a poison we drink hoping it will kill someone else.

Don't sow to lying. "Wherefore, putting away lying, speak every man truth with his neighbor; for we are members one of another" (Eph. 4:25). You will most likely reap a hard heart, seared conscience, loss of friends, naivety, and paranoia.

Don't sow to pride, greed, jealousy, gossip, an undisciplined life, hatred, envy, apathy, cowardice, discord, witchcraft, rebellion, or intoxicants.

Don't sow to unbelief or you will reap a crop of doubts and cynicism. It is reported that an atheist who took his own life, once said, "Life is just a dirty trick, a short journey from nothingness to nothingness. There is no remedy for anything in life. Man's destiny in the universe is like a colony of ants on a burning log."

SOWING TO THE SPIRIT

Sowing is a doing thing. If you leave the seed in the barn there will be no harvest. If you do nothing with the seeds of spiritual things, you can't expect any fruit. Jesus said, "And why call ye me Lord, Lord, and do not the things which I say?" (Lk. 6:46). James challenges the early Church with this clear exhortation: "But be ye doers of the word and not hearers only, deceiving your own selves. For if any be a hearer of the word, and not a doer, he is like a man beholding his natural face in a mirror; for he beholdeth himself, and goeth his way, and immediately forgetteth what manner of man he was. But whosoever looketh into the perfect law of liberty, and continueth in it, he being not a forgetful hearer but a doer of the work, this man shall be blessed in his deed" (Jas. 1:22–25).

The Word of God is a spiritual seed in itself. In book three of this series, "By The Word Of God", I wrote on the importance of the Bible in our daily lives. I tried to emphasize that even in the chapter titles: Read It Daily, Study It Carefully, Memorize It Intentionally, Meditate On It Continually, Share It Lovingly, and Obey It Passionately. When Jesus taught on the parable of the sower His disciples asked Him the meaning. The first thing He told them was, "Now the parable is this; The seed is the word of God" (Lk. 8:11). The more you sow to the Word of God the more direction you have for your life. "Thy word is a lamp unto my feet, and a light unto my path" (Ps. 119:105). There is a deep and abiding peace that settles over the soul of the one who loves the Word. "Great peace have they who love thy law, and nothing shall offend them" (Ps. 119:165).

Sow to prayer, especially private prayer. Jesus said to go into your closet and shut the door and pray to your Father Who is in secret and your Father Who seeth in secret shall reward you openly. Private prayer is the greatest expression of your Christian faith. Who you are when you are alone in prayer with God is who you truly are, nothing more. Men ought always to pray and not to faint. If God were to say to me He would never answer another prayer of mine, I would still pray because entering into His presence is a cure for most all the anxiousness of my soul. "Be anxious for nothing, but in everything, by prayer and supplication with thanksgiving, let your requests be made know unto God. And the peace of God, which passeth all understanding, shall keep your hearts and minds through Christ Jesus" (Phil. 4:6–7).

Sow to self-denial. "And he said to them all, If any man will come after me, let him deny himself, and take up his cross daily, and follow me" (Lk. 9:23). The secret to anger resolution is to yield my rights. In my morning prayers I have 32 rights that I yield every day. Anger is evidence to me that I have taken my rights back. Where the Spirit of the Lord is there is liberty and grace to help in time of need.

Sow to humility. Jesus said if a man exalts himself, he shall be abased but if he humbles himself, he shall be exalted. It is impossible to offend a humble person. "In like manner, ye younger, submit yourselves unto the elder. Yea, all of you be subject one to another, and be clothed with humility; for God resisteth the proud, and giveth grace to the humble. Humble yourselves, therefore, under the mighty hand of God, that he may exalt you in due time" (1Pet. 5:5–6). Every time I try to exalt myself in the eyes of my wife and family, it fails; but every time I humble myself, God lifts me up. Sow to the Spirit and He will produce fruit in your life that only He can. "But the fruit of the Spirit is love, joy, peace, long-suffering, gentleness, goodness, faith, meekness, self-control; against such there is no law" (Gal.5:22–23)

THE DRY BONES COME TO LIFE

In some ways the coming together of the dry bones in Ezekiel's vision is like the spiritual disciplines in progressive sanctification. At the beginning there is only the promise of breath and life. This is the Word preached when the Holy Spirit begins the work in a heart and there starts a shaking and the bones come together. Then the sinew and flesh and skin follow. As completed bodies fill the valley, there is one thing lacking: breath! The hand of the Lord was in it from beginning to end but it involved the obedience of the prophet for it to be accomplished. In the same way our sanctification, though a work of the Spirit from beginning to end, must involve our participation. When Ezekiel was asked by the Spirit if these bones could live, he answered, "O Lord God, thou knowest." He was commanded to preach the Word in a seemingly hopeless situation and simply trust God with what would happen.

I am aware the context of Ezekiel's vision is announcing the restoration of the nation of Israel which began to be fulfilled May 14th, 1948, and continues to be fulfilled even to this day. I have chosen to include the text to illustrate in some way the similarity between the process of spiritual disciplines and the need for the breath of the Holy Spirit to bring things to life.

CHAPTER SIX

The Spirit's Witness in Worship

Man was made to enjoy worshipping his Maker. In true worship we understand our origin and destiny, our meaning and purpose. This is only one of the many blessings of true worship. If man does not worship the one true God, he will worship and serve something else, usually the works of his own hands. He will bow down, do obeisance, pay homage and even show reverence to the things he has made. As long as he can worship the things he has made he is in control. Because of the blindness of sin, man unknowingly directs worship toward himself. When he exchanges the truth of God for a lie, he worships and serves the creature more than the creator. If true worship is going to occur, it must involve the Person and work of the Holy Spirit. "But the hour cometh, and now is, when the true worshipers shall worship the Father in spirit and in truth; for the Father seeketh such to worship him. God is a Spirit; and they that worship him must worship him in spirit and in truth" (Jn. 4:23–24).

In 1990 as I was studying this passage in John 4, I asked

myself the question: "have I ever worshiped God in spirit and in truth?" For the next two years I would study and preach from this passage many times. In fact my favorite gospel sermon to date is "The woman at the well." She is the first person to whom Jesus clearly told Who He was. Was He worthy of worship? She believed He was. She left her water pot, went and told the town she had found the Messiah. I began to read books on worship; three of my favorites are:

WHATEVER HAPPENED TO WORSHIP by A.W.Tozer
TRUE WORSHIP by Warren Wiersbe
HOW TO WORSHIP JESUS CHRIST, by Joseph S. Carroll

During those two years, I would read the words, "Worship Service", in church bulletins which was generally followed by the order of service. I would hear worship leaders say, "Let's stand for worship" and they would lead in some great songs. I began to sow spiritual seeds of personal worship by telling the Lord at the beginning of my morning prayers that I loved Him and worshiped Him. Sometimes I would silently sing a hymn of praise or worship to the Lord. After about a two year journey of desiring true worship I woke one morning at my usual time of 5:00am. I began my prayers and sensed the still small voice of the Holy Spirit telling me to get dressed and go up on the barn roof. I gave a number of reasons why this couldn't be God, but eventually I concluded it was early enough that no one would see me. As I got up on the roof, I looked toward the east and it was first light. The sky was clear and the blue of dawn was mixing with the grey of the fading night. I could see the whole moon but only a thin slice of it was white. Directly beneath it was the morning star shining brightly. The temperature was cool and yet somehow I felt balmy as a light breeze blew across my face. As I stood there enjoying the beauty of the moment the Word of the Lord came to me: "When I consider thy heavens, the works of thy fingers, the moon and the stars, which thou hast ordained, what is man, that thou art mindful of him? And the son of man, that thou visitest him?" (Ps. 8:3–4). I laid down on the roof for about twenty or thirty minutes and in speechless adoration sensed the presence of God. I felt cleansed, renewed, restored, and revived. I felt as if I had truly worshiped God in a way I never had before.

The next morning I awoke and asked the Lord if He wanted me to get on the barn roof again. I have never had Him tell me to get up there again. Oh, I've been up there but I've never sensed Him telling me to go. I learned two things about worship that has helped me tremendously. First, worship in spirit and in truth can occur spontaneously. Secondly, it cannot be programmed into my computer and be repeated by typing it onto my schedule and expecting it to come up on the screen. I have had many such private worship experiences since then. I am humbled and strengthened in my faith each time though the context is not the same. Sometimes while setting at my desk studying Scripture I will be overcome with joy in the Lord. Sometimes while driving my car I will burst into a spiritual song singing to God and making melody in my heart to Him. Sometimes in the back yard I'll catch the fragrance of fresh mowed grass and be carried away in worship of my Maker. A sunset, a star-filled night, the first robin in the spring, a wave on the sea, a glance from my wife, the thought of my family, a walk, a friend, rain, snow, wind or calm, even a hardship can bring about true worship of my Maker and my Sustainer.

IT'S NOT *WHERE* YOU WORSHIP, BUT WHO AND *HOW*

The woman at the well wanted to follow the tradition of the Samaritans and worship in the place of her fathers. She took issue with the Jews who said that Jerusalem was the only proper place to worship God. Jesus made it very clear that the place was not important. True worship is about who you worship and how you worship them. If you worship the Father in spirit and in truth, you can do it in a corn field.

In the wilderness, Satan tempted Christ to worship him. The devil offered Him all the kingdoms of the world and the glory of them if He would fall down and worship him. Jesus made it clear that God alone was worthy of worship. "Then sayeth Jesus unto him, Begone, Satan; for it is written, Thou shalt worship the Lord, thy God, and him only shalt thou serve" (Mt. 4:10). When Jesus said, It is written, He referred to the Scripture and the God of Scripture; the only true God and His Son; the Almighty God, Creator, Sustainer, Maker of heaven and earth. The God of Scripture is in a class all His own. There is no God beside Him. Knowing the Scripture is a must if we are ever to know the One we must worship.

To worship in spirit and truth must include the heart. Jesus quoted Isaiah 29:13 when dealing with the hypocrisy of the Scribes and Pharisees. "This people draweth near unto me with their mouth, and honoreth me with their lips, but their heart is far from me. But in vain they do worship me, teaching for doctrines the commandments of men" (Mt. 15:8–9). The word "vain" means something which appears to have value, but in reality has none. The Scribes and Pharisees had a form of godliness but denied the power of it. The power of true worship comes from the Spirit bearing witness with our spirit. Worship is a spiritual experience. It is possible to be at a corporate worship service with people who are truly worshiping and not experience worship yourself. Private worship is what enhances corporate worship. It is that spontaneous private worship which brings people to full assurance of faith and a walk of nearness to the Lord. I think so many people doubt their salvation and see so little fruit in their lives because they have not experienced true worship in the Spirit. Being an itinerant preacher I meet Christians regularly for the first time. Some of them I feel a kindred spirit with almost immediately. As I get to know them better one thing seems to stand out: they have a heartfelt love and worship of God. They speak highly of Him with adoring words from a countenance that radiates adoration. The witness of the Spirit is in them and the grace of the Spirit is about them. I know the language here is very subjective and thus vulnerable to all sorts of criticism, but the language of the heart risks criticism.

Faithful Men of Michigan

In the autumn of 1993 I was so moved by what I was learning about worship that I wanted to share it with a group of men. I asked 24 men from all kinds of denominational backgrounds to meet with me at a local township hall. Most of these men were strangers to each other but the one thing they all had in common was a genuine faith in Christ and a sincere love for Him. Many of these men drove for well over an hour to attend. We committed to meet for two hours on Thursday nights for a three month period. Some of the men were pastors, some college students, and even one high school student (our sixteen year old son, Brian). Most of them were working men with families. During the first hour we would divide into pairs for quoting our Scripture memory assignment. We committed to memorize 2 Cor. 4. Then we would have a short study on a basic doctrine, a basic concept, or a basic responsibility. It was made clear that our main purpose was to worship the Lord. So while we met in a conference room for the first part of the meeting, we would move into the larger hall for worship. Each man would find a place around the walls usually spaced ten to fifteen feet apart. We shut off the main lights but the exits lights were more than adequate. The first few moments were usually spent in silence. Eventually someone would pray as they felt led by the Lord. Many times prayer broke out in unison, each man praying in a low tone just above a whisper. Sometimes it was quiet until a man would recite Scripture or give praise to God for His goodness. Sometimes a man would come under conviction and repent of a sin asking for special prayer. Many times someone would quote a portion of Scripture followed by another and another as though we were listening to a powerful message being preached by the Spirit of God. There were times a man might break into a hymn and every man would join in singing. Men had the liberty to stand, sit, lift their hands or keep them in their pockets. No two meetings were identical yet each one had its unique blessing. The hour for worship seemed to pass quickly and many times we didn't want to leave. These were truly faithful men. At the end of three months we didn't want to stop. We took three months off to see what the Lord might do. At the end of the three month break there were six groups started from these original men. I wondered what the Lord might do with our efforts over a seven year season. The seven year course was set. At the end of that time there were over fifty groups involving some 2000 men. Sowing to worship in those days continues to produce spiritual fruit in my life today and many of those faithful men echo the same.

Worship and Praise

Praise is the language spoken from a heart of worship. David wrote more praises to God than any other penmen of Scripture. He was a man who loved God and longed to have a heart clean before Him. As the Spirit of God moved him to write, he would bless and praise God. It was a purposeful act of his will. "I will bless the Lord at all times; his praise shall continually be in my mouth. My soul shall make her boast in the Lord; the humble shall hear of it, and be glad. Oh, magnify the Lord with me, and let us exalt his name together. I sought the Lord, and he heard me, and delivered me from all my fears" (Ps. 34:1–4). David was accustomed to dwelling in the presence of God enjoying times of spiritual worship and praise. He even danced before the Lord in public at the thought of having the ark in Jerusalem. He praised the Lord in the great congregation as well as in private. He even praised God in the night seasons. The fear of sin stealing these precious times was of great concern to him. After Nathan's confrontation about his sin with Bathsheba, he begged God not to cast him away from His presence, not to take the Holy Spirit from him. How could he have spiritual worship and praise without the Spirit? Worship and praise from a pure heart is always an acceptable sacrifice to God. This true worship and praise strengthens, establishes, and settles us in our faith.

Worship and Song

Christians are known for their singing and their songs. One of my hobbies is collecting hymnals and song books. Over the years I have limited myself to about two hundred of them. They contain many songs written to the Lord and many about the Lord's greatness. For the most part they mirror some scriptural theme. God's blessed plan of redemption is especially prevalent. I have heard it said that when you hear people singing, you will know what they believe. I think that is a great truth. Singing is one of the evidences of Spirit-filled Christians: "Speaking to yourselves in psalms and hymns and spiritual songs, singing and making melody in your heart to the Lord, giving thanks always for all things unto God and the Father in the name of our Lord Jesus Christ" (Eph. 5:19–20). Sometimes singing or thanksgiving leads me into worship and sometimes worship leads me into singing and thanksgiving. Either way it's the Holy Spirit that leads me into true spiritual worship.

WORSHIP AND PRAYER

One of the precious names of the Holy Spirit is the Comforter, the One called alongside to help. We are told to pray in the Holy Spirit. "Praying always with all prayer and supplication in the Spirit, and watching thereunto with all perseverance and supplications for all saints" (Eph. 6:18). You can worship in all kinds of prayer when the Holy Spirit is helping you. Prayer can be work: "Epapharas, who is one of you, a servant of Christ, greeteth you, always laboring fervently for you in prayers, that ye may stand perfect and complete in all the will of God" (Col. 4:12). One's faith can be built up when praying in the Holy Spirit. "But ye, beloved, building up yourselves on your most holy faith, praying in the Holy Spirit" (Jude 20). Worship can occur when we receive help from the Holy Spirit during prayer. In the same way Jesus intercedes for us when we sin, the Holy Spirit makes intercessions for us when we pray. Prayer is something every saint needs and every saint needs the Holy Spirit's help when they pray. "Likewise, the Spirit also helpeth our infirmity; for we know not what we should pray for as we ought; but the Spirit himself maketh intercession for us with groanings which cannot be uttered. And he that searcheth the hearts knoweth what is the mind of the Spirit, because he maketh intercession for the saints according to the will of God" (Rom. 8:26–27). Many times when praying for people and circumstances that are beyond my control, true worship occurs and the fruit of the Spirit fills my soul with multiplied grace and peace.

What a blessed thought to know our heavenly Father seeketh such to worship Him. Oh how we need the help of the Holy Spirit in all we do. It pleases the Father to help us for God did not create us to be independent from Him but totally dependent on Him.

WORSHIP AND THE SPIRITUAL MAN

The Holy Spirit is the One who makes a man spiritual. A spiritual man is one who is born of God; he operates off grace, produces righteousness, glorifies God and is approved of by God. The natural man is born of the flesh, he operates off the Law, produces self-righteousness, glorifies man, and is approved of by man. The natural man cannot see the spiritual things for they seem foolish to him. "But the natural man receiveth not the things of the Spirit of God; for they are foolishness unto him, neither can he know them, because they are spiritually discerned. But he that is spiritual judgeth all things, yet he himself is judged of no man. For who hath known the mind of the Lord, that he may instruct him? But we have the mind of Christ" (1Cor. 2:14–16). It is impossible to understand true worship without the Person and work of the Holy Spirit. It would be like trying to describe a beautiful sunset to a man who had been born blind. Glory and honor, majesty and praise to the Father of our Lord Jesus Christ for sending the Holy Spirit to help us in our worship.

EARS TO HEAR GOD'S VOICE

It's hard to imagine that only seven years ago I began the project of writing these books. I wanted to write seven: one a year for seven years. My main purpose was to leave a legacy of faith for our children and grandchildren. I wanted to leave them a written record of what Joyce and I feel are the essentials in their journey of faith. Sermons are all too quickly forgotten but maybe a few short books could be used to encourage them, even after we are gone. We also realized that something left on paper is one way to live after you are dead. It is hard to imagine that I am beginning the last chapter of the last book, and quite honestly, I feel somewhat overcome with gratefulness and humility. The Lord is good. Bless and praise His Holy Name! Seven years ago this conclusion seemed so far away. It is a reminder of the passing of time and the brevity of life. Writing has not come easy to me; however, my precious wife has stood by me and encouraged me to press on. I will forever be in her debt for she is a faithful and godly wife. It is a joy to love her and be heirs together with her of the grace of life.

The Language of the Spirit

I believe it is possible to hear the words of Scripture without hearing the voice of God, as the book title states, "The Spirit Himself Beareth Witness". The Holy Spirit is the voice of God who speaks the language which communicates to the spirit of a man. The Jews, more than any other people, heard the words of Scripture but many times they missed or ignored the voice of His Spirit. They were the people with the greatest advantage, for the best means of hearing the Spirit's voice is in hearing the words of Scripture. Hearing the Scriptures was good but hearing His voice in the Scriptures would have been better. "Search the scriptures; for in them ye think ye have eternal life; and they are they which testify of me. And ye will not come to me, that ye might have life" (Jn. 5:39–40). Oh what a blessing to hear the life giving voice of His Spirit in the Scriptures. "It is the spirit that giveth life; the flesh profiteth nothing. The words that I speak unto you, they are spirit, and they are life "(Jn. 6:63).

Poorly preached sermons become powerful when anointed by the Spirit of God; and exegetically perfect sermons are lifeless without the witness of the Holy Spirit. The Word of God is living and powerful because of the Spirit who inspired it. "For the prophecy came not at any time by the will of man, but holy men of God spoke as they were moved by the Holy Spirit" (2Pet. 1:21). Wicked men have twisted the words of Scripture, even Satan himself has quoted it. "Then the devil taketh him up into the holy city, and setteth him on a pinnacle of the temple, and saith unto him, If thou be the Son of God, cast thyself down; for it is written, He shall give his angels charge concerning thee, and in their hands they shall bear thee up, lest at any time thou dash thy foot against a stone" (Mt. 4:5–6). The power of Scripture lay in the witness of the One who inspired it.

THE SPIRIT OF A MAN

When God made man and formed him of the dust of the ground, he lay there lifeless until God breathed life into him. This breath of life was a life-giving spirit similar to the Spirit of God. It was not in His exact likeness for God is not confined to a body like man; but in the sense that we are a spirit, we were made in His likeness. The life of the body is dependent on that spirit remaining in the body. When the spirit of a man departs the body, the body dies and goes back to dust until the day of resurrection when the spirit and the body will once again reunite.

The Holy Spirit bears witness with the spirit of a man and gives him understanding of Who God is, and what God's desire is for him. The life-giving breath of the Holy Spirit is referred to as illumination. "But there is a spirit in man; and the inspiration of the Almighty giveth them understanding" (Job 32:8). Solomon writes of the spirit of a man as being the light of the Lord that reveals the inner workings of his soul. "The spirit of man is the lamp of the Lord, searching all the inward parts" (Prov. 20:27). Knowledge of God comes from the Holy Spirit to our spirit. Our relationship with God is a spiritual one which radiates to every fiber of our heart, mind, soul, and strength. "For what man knoweth the things of a man, except the spirit of man which is in him? Even so the things of God knoweth no man, but the Spirit of God. Now we have received, not the spirit of the world, but the Spirit who is of God; that we might know the things that are freely given to us of God" (1Cor. 2:11–12). A person who is born again is spiritually alive. God dwells in him and bears witness with his spirit. The Holy Spirit leads him in the way he should go. The remaining pages of this chapter will be focused on learning to hear and discern His guiding voice.

He That Hath An Ear

There have been times when people have been speaking to me and for some reason I was distracted and no longer listening. Oh I am hearing their voice but not listening to their words. At times Joyce will be talking to me, I may even be looking her in the eye, and she will realize I am not listening to a word she is saying. I feel bad when she catches me in that condition because it seems to make her feel like what she is saying is not important. It's not that I have a sinister plot not to listen I just get distracted with less important things than hearing her words. As we have grown older we have worked on the art of listening to each other with more than just the natural ear. I wonder if that's what Jesus had in mind when He addressed the issue of ears and hearing. "He that hath ears to hear, let him hear" (Mt. 11:15). He encourages listeners with this statement in several different situations and sometimes repeatedly for emphasis. I believe the breakdown in hearing His voice or the witness of the Spirit lay in our spiritual ears.

Ears That Don't Hear

Throughout the Old Testament the Lord would send prophets to His people to speak to them the Word of the Lord. The Holy Spirit would bear witness and some would gratefully obey His voice but often the majority would resist His Spirit. This same problem was present during the days of Jesus' ministry. For this reason He often spoke to the masses in parables. A parable contained a mystery previously hidden which was now being divinely revealed. Many times Jesus would use an earthly story with a heavenly meaning for those who had ears to hear. When His disciples asked Him why He did this, He made this response. "And the disciples came, and said unto him, Why speakest thou unto them in parables? He answered and said unto them, Because it is given unto you to know the mysteries of the kingdom of heaven, but to them it is not given. For whosoever hath, to him shall be given, and he shall have more abundance; but whosoever hath not, from him shall be taken away even what he hath. Therefore speak I to them in parables, because they seeing, see not; and hearing, they hear not, neither do they understand. And in them is fulfilled the prophecy of Isaiah, which saith, By hearing, ye shall hear and shall not understand; and seeing, ye shall see and shall not perceive; for this people's heart is become gross, and their ears are dull of hearing, and their eyes they have closed, lest at any time they should see with their eyes, and hear with their ears, and should understand with their heart, and should be converted, and I should heal them" (Mt. 13:10–15). As the people heard the inspired words of the prophets of God, they quenched the voice of God's Spirit and closed their spiritual ears. Disobedience to the voice of God's Spirit will eventually bring about deafness to the value of spiritual things.

In Stephen's final message he addresses ears that don't hear: "Ye stiff-necked and uncircumcised in heart and ears, ye do always resist the Holy Spirit; as your fathers did, so do ye. Which of the prophets have not your fathers persecuted? And they have slain them who showed before of the coming of the Just One, of whom ye have been now the betrayers and murderers; Who have received the law by the disposition of angels, and have not kept it" (Acts 7:51–53). The spiritual heart of a man and the spiritual ears of a man are inseparably attached to one another. A circumcised heart is one that has cut away the callousness of arrogant resistance to God's Spirit. Circumcised ears are ones that are turned toward heaven and desire a word from the Lord. On many occasions I have said to the Lord, "if You have something to say to me, I want to hear it." If I am serious I will add, "and I will obey what You say to me." He has been faithful to speak when I have ears to hear and a heart to obey.

DISCERNING GOD'S VOICE

Over the years Joyce and I have developed an ear for one another's voice. Often times we can even pick out each other's voice in a crowd. Sometimes when searching for her in the grocery store, all I have to do is mildly clear my throat and she will know it is me. There are a lot of voices coming at us and it's not always easy to know which one is God's. The voices of the world bombard us. Many times it's obvious by the content of the message that it is not of God. Sometimes it's a little more subtle and less easy to discern. Then there is the voice of the devil, the father of lies, the master deceiver; yes, he too speaks to the spirit of our mind. Then there is our own voice. Nobody talks to me more than me. It is a common problem for me and possibly a problem to more people than want to admit it. I will ask the Lord to speak to me about something and find myself talking to myself. Then I'm stuck wondering if it is God or me. I have learned to run a simple test that, over the years, has helped me discern if the voice is God's or not. I wouldn't say it is foolproof, but it has certainly been of service to me in my journey of faith.

The idea of a test was impressed on me from the following Scripture: "Beloved, believe not every spirit, but test the spirits whether they are of God; because many false prophets are gone out into the world. By this know ye the Spirit of God; every spirit that confesseth that Jesus Christ is come in the flesh is of God; and every spirit that confesseth not that Jesus Christ is come in the flesh is not of God; and this is that spirit of antichrist, of which ye have heard that it should come, and even now already is in the world. Ye are of God, little children, and have overcome them, because greater is he that is in you, than he that is in the world. They are of the world; therefore speak they of the world, and the world heareth them. We are of God. He that knoweth God heareth us; he that is not of God heareth not us. By this know we the spirit of truth, and the spirit of error" (1Jn. 4:1–6).

The first questions I ask myself in attempting to discern the voice of God is: "Does it glorify God? Will obeying the voice bring glory to God?" "Whether, therefore, ye eat, or drink, or whatever ye do, do all to the glory of God" (1Cor. 10:31); "Being filled with the fruits of righteousness, which are by Jesus Christ, unto the glory and praise of God" (Phil. 1:11). The Holy Spirit would never tell me to do something that would bring shame or reproach on His name. Jesus said when the Spirit of truth would come He would glorify the Son. "He shall glorify me; for he shall receive of mine, and shall show it unto you" (Jn. 16:14). The Holy Spirit is on constant alert to my attempts at self-glorification. He speaks clearly to my spirit on the subject. If the voice I hear is for the glory of God, my spiritual ears are tuned to listen further.

The second question is, "If I obey the voice, would it result in something good?" David knew the Lord was good by nature and out of His essence He would do good. "Oh, taste and see that the Lord is good; blessed is the man who trusteth in him" (Ps. 34:8). Jesus was anointed by God for the purpose of doing good. Peter spoke of "How God anointed Jesus of Nazareth with the Holy Spirit, and with power; who went about doing good, and healing all that were oppressed of the devil; for God was with him" (Acts 10:38). There have been numerous occasions when the Holy Spirit has led me in the path of doing good in the face of evil. I have recognized the voice of His Spirit to mine in the words of the Apostle Paul. "Be not overcome by evil, but overcome evil with good" (Rom. 12:21). When I hear a voice telling me to overcome evil with more evil, I quickly discern it is not the voice of the Holy Spirit. If I ever hear a voice of revenge against those who do me wrong, I can count on it not being from God. "Dearly beloved, avenge not yourselves but, rather, give place unto wrath; for it is written, Vengeance is mine; I will repay, sayeth the Lord" (Rom. 12:19). Saved or lost, all people have an inner sense from God of right and wrong, good and evil. As the child of God develops an ear to hear the witness of the Spirit, it will always be a voice zealous of good works. "Who gave himself for us that he might redeem us from all iniquity, and purify unto himself a people of his own, zealous of good works." (Ti. 2:14)

The third question I ask when I hear a voice is, "Does what it is saying line up with Scripture?" God will never command us to do something He has forbidden in Scripture. A pastor once told me he had lost his affections for his wife and felt affections for another woman in his church. He sensed the Lord was telling him to divorce his wife and marry the other woman. I looked him in the eyes and told him clearly, that is not the voice of God, for God had already spoken in Scripture. "The Pharisees also came unto him, testing him, and saying unto him, Is it lawful for a man to put away his wife for every cause? And he answered and said unto them, Have ye not read that he who made them at the beginning, made them male and female; and said, For this cause shall a man leave father and mother, and shall cleave to his wife, and they two shall be one flesh? Wherefore, they are no more two, but one flesh. What, therefore, God hath joined together, let not man put asunder" (Mt. 19:3–6). God has already spoken on many topics and He will not so much as whisper a word to the contrary. He will never speak an endorsing word in favor of malice, deceit, hypocrisies, envies, gossip, pride, lust, covetousness, greed, and the like for He has already spoken on these subjects and more in Scripture.

DEVELOPING SPIRITUAL EARS

Every year I choose a spiritual goal. I have done this since 1979. It has been a good spiritual exercise for me. My goal this year is to develop ears to hear what the Holy Spirit is saying to my spirit. Every day I pray to be filled with the Holy Spirit. To be filled with the Holy Spirit means to be controlled by Him. Hearing the voice of God in the midst of all the other voices that want to control us requires finely tuned spiritual ears; ears that are closely connected to the control center of our heart. I wish to conclude this last book with two considerations on developing spiritual ears.

HEARING PROTECTION

I have some hearing loss because I didn't wear sufficient ear protection while spending hours behind a chain saw. Then there is mowing the lawn, tilling the garden, firearms, skill saws, and just being a citizen of a noisy mechanized culture. If I had taken better care to wear ear plugs or some form of hearing protection I might have saved some of my ability to hear. I also need to wear spiritual hearing protection. I don't have to listen to the lies of the devil. Regardless of how persistent or how loud his lies are I don't have to listen to them. My ears are not garbage buckets for satanic waste. In the beginning Satan called God a liar and accused Him in front of the first man and woman. Adam should have refused to listen and instead told him to be gone.

I have listened to some things I wish I had never heard. Words plant thoughts and lying words can damage sensitivity to spiritual ears and one's ability to hear truth, just as the drone of a chain saw has stolen sensitivity to hear the voices of those I love. I have learned not to listen to certain things; things like gossip, lies against creation, lies about marriage or morals, or lies spoken against Biblical virtue. When a culture declares war on virtue it is because they have listened to lies so long they begin to believe them. A culture can quickly become deaf to the Spirit of truth with ears that are only open to hearing lies. It is by the Word of God that we can discern the Spirit of truth and the spirit of error. It is especially important in these last days to use care in what we listen to. "For the time will come when they will not endure sound doctrine but, after their own lusts, shall they heap to themselves teachers, having itching ears; and they shall turn away their ears from the truth, and shall be turned unto fables" (2Tim. 4:3–4).

As Moses was giving the Law to the children of Israel he told them to be circumspect in everything they heard. He goes on to say, "don't even mention the name of other gods." Why would he tell them to not even mention their names? They have just left a culture where they had been bombarded with hearing the names and claims of the false gods of Egypt. They were to come out of idolatry. Remember, Moses wasn't even gone a full 40 days when they began demanding Aaron to make them a golden calf, a request with which he was too quick to comply. There is great protection in being circumspect; a man may ruin himself with mere carelessness. On the other hand it requires precision and attention to detail to preserve something as precious as one's faith. "And in all these things that I have said unto you be circumspect: and make no mention of the name of other gods, neither let it be heard out of thy mouth" (Ex. 23:13). An affirming word from Paul to the church at Ephesus: "See, then, that ye walk circumspectly, not as fools but as wise, redeeming the time, because the days are evil" (Eph. 5:15–16). O be careful little ears what you hear.

STILLNESS

It is hard to find stillness in our noisy world. The quietest places we have ever found were in the wilderness areas of Alaska. We left the typical noisy sounds of Anchorage and headed toward the Wrangell Mountain range. The scenery was breathtaking as we stopped at a scenic turnoff and shut off the car. We hadn't seen another car for some time, no planes overhead, and there wasn't a sound—just the stillness. We both noticed it immediately and simultaneously made the same remark, "The silence seems almost deafening." We couldn't remember when or if we had ever experienced complete stillness. We stood there speechless soaking up the beauty of the moment. We wondered if this was what David meant when he said, "Be still, and know that I am God" (Ps.46:10a).

Finding a still place to have your quiet time with God is not easy, but it is possible. Turn off as much competition as you can: the television, radio, phones, any mechanical noise makers or eye catchers. You can hear God while on the move, but I have found I am more likely to hear His voice when I purposely stop and intentionally listen. "Stand in awe, and sin not; commune with your own heart upon your bed, and be still. Selah" (Ps. 4:4). The word "stand" used here carries with it the idea of becoming stationary, as does lying in bed. I think the Psalmist may be trying to emphasize the fact that it's best to stop moving.

I have been in a hurry most of my life. I eat fast, dress fast, talk fast, and walk fast. I'm driven from one project to another, always in a hurry to get something done so I can begin the next thing. In this mad dash I fear I have missed hearing God's voice on many occasions. Many of the tasks are good and need to be done, but the driven pace has been brutal on my spiritual ears. I am learning to slow down because it's become obvious to me that when I am in a hurry, I am almost always in the flesh. When I am in the flesh, I don't listen well to others and least of all to the Spirit of God. God is never in a hurry. If I want to keep pace with Him and hear the voice of His Spirit, I must slow down and listen. David learned how to stop and listen for the Lord's voice. When he was in a hurry he was impatient and almost always made mistakes. When he waited on the Lord though, he received direction and deliverance from the consequences of spiritual deafness. "I waited patiently for the Lord, and he inclined unto me, and heard my cry. He brought me up also out of an horrible pit, out of the miry clay, and set my feet upon a rock, and established my goings. And he hath put a new song in my mouth, even praise unto our God; many shall see it, and fear, and shall trust in the Lord. Blessed is the man who maketh the Lord his trust, and respecteth not the proud, nor such as turn aside to lies. Many, O Lord, my God, are thy wonderful works which thou hast done, and thy thoughts which are toward us; they cannot be reckoned up in order unto thee. If I would declare and speak them, they are more than can be numbered" (Ps. 40:1–5). My ability to hear with my spiritual ears is improving as I slow down. The goal is to stop and be still which is the best posture for His Spirit to bear witness with my spirit that I am a child of God

DEDICATION AND PRAYER

These books are dedicated to our precious children and grandchildren. You were in our hearts when we began this book project and remain there to their completion and beyond. We love you and are so thankful to God for you and all He has done and is doing in your lives. We pray the essential truths in these books will be a source of encouragement and strength as you press on in your journey of faith.

We thank God for you and pray for you every day. We joyfully make request to God on your behalf. We pray your love would abound in the knowledge of God and that you would make wise judgments. We pray you would remain steadfast in the Lord without offense until the day of Christ. We pray your lives would be filled with the fruits of righteousness by the power of the indwelling Spirit of God. May you live in such a way as to bring glory and praise to God. We pray that He would give you the spirit of wisdom and revelation as you read and study the Scriptures. May He give you a mind that understands truth and a heart that readily applies it. May you become mighty men and women of prayer and faith, strong in the Lord and the power of His might. May you become rooted and grounded in your love for God and each other. May you be filled with all spiritual understanding. May you have patience and long-suffering with joyfulness all your days. May the Lord protect you from the evil one and keep you from the spirit of antichrist that is in the philosophies of the world. We pray if you have to suffer for the Name of Christ that you not be ashamed but experience the Spirit of glory and of God resting upon you. May you establish good godly homes. May you find mates that would enhance your walk with God, not diminish it. We pray that you would love the Word of God and hide His Word in your hearts. May you always be about the business of working out your own salvation with a deep abiding reverence for that which is holy. May you live a quiet and peaceable life in all godliness and honesty. May the peace of God which passes all understanding keep your hearts and minds in Christ Jesus all the days of your journey, in the Almighty Name of Jesus Christ, Amen.

CPSIA information can be obtained
at www.ICGtesting.com
Printed in the USA
FFOW05n1733300615